7/6/98

Bavarian Cooking

assembled by Olli Leeb

Title of German Language Edition: "Bayerische Leibspeisen"
English Translation: Maria Rerrich, Munich

1997 8th Edition   ISBN 3-921799-85-6

© Kochbuchverlag Olli Leeb,   D-80687 Munich
Printed by: Walter Biering GmbH   Munich
Illustrations: Kerrin v. Carnap   Icking
               Susanne Becker   Munich
Photos: p. 17 Klaus Broszat   Munich
               p. 35/127/145/158 P. C. Fischer   Baldham
               p. 73 Foto Berger   Munich
               p. 91/109 meine Familie und ich, Burda Munich
               p. 163 Studio Teubner   Füssen
Binding: R. Oldenbourg   Heimstetten

Printed in Germany

Contents

Foreword

ords of encouragement spoken by a bookseller have led to the creation of this book. It is meant above all for English-speaking tourists who enjoyed their visit to our country, and who would like to take just under 1 lb of *Bavaria* back home with them - that is what the book was to weigh at the most, so as not to make it too heavy for any-one's luggage, probably burdened down already with a 4 lb. souvenir beermug.

This book should, of course, say something about Bavaria, about the people and the customs, about the specialties served in restaurants and, above all, about Bavarian home cooking, to make it possible for you to prepare at home what you liked here. This desire awakens mostly when holiday memories are rekindled. Since the simple ingredients of Bavarian cooking are available in every country of the temperate zone, it should certainly not be difficult to recreate your particular favorite dish.

This is a collection of old family recipes, updated by the addition of new data for cooking times and temperatures.

I hope you will have a good time cooking the Bavarian way, and wish you the best of success.

A Few Words About Bavaria

When you arrive at the Bavarian border and read the sign "Freistaat Bayern" (Free State of Bavaria), it is a good thing to know that you are about to enter a country of extraordinary beauty.

As early as 1,200 years ago the first Bavarian author, Arbeo, Bishop of Freising, wrote this about Bavaria and its inhabitants:

"It was very good, lovely to look at, rich in groves, and well provided with wine.It possessed iron in abundance;gold,silver and purple were plentiful.Its men were tall and strong and there excisted charity and human compassion. The soil was fertile and produced rich harvests.The ground seemed almost totally covered with cattle and herds of all kinds. There was truly an immense quantity of honey and bees,as well as innumerable fishes in lakes and rivers.Clear wells and brooks watered the land;it had what it needed by way of salt.The capital,Regensburg,was impregnable, built of square blocks ... The hill country was rich in fruit and offered pastures and juicy grass.The mountain forests were popu- lated by wild animals, and the undergrowth by deer,elks,bison, roe deer,wild goats ..." *

The wild animals have disappeared -- but the lovely,varied countryside has remained,with its hospitable and likeable people.

Today,Bavaria is the largest state of the Federal Republic of Germany.It is twice the size of Switzerland.One-third of its territory is covered with forests.As you can see on the map bound into this book,Bavaria is divided into the following areas:

Altbayern
(Old Bavaria)   (or Altbaiern) with the governmental districts of Oberpfalz (Upper Palatinate) in the North-East, Niederbayern (Lower Bavaria) in the South-East,and Oberbayern (Upper Bavaria) in the South,

Franken
(Franconia)   with Ober- Mittel- and Unterfranken (Upper- Central- and Lower Franconia) in the North,and

Schwaben
(Swabia)   with Bayrisch-Schwaben (Bavarian Swabia) and the Allgäu region in the South-West.

*(L.Schott:Herrscher Bayerns,1974.D-Munich,Süddeutscher Verlag).

Despite the widely differing character of the individual regions, they all have one thing in common: the beauty of the countryside. Upper Bavaria, with its picturesque towns and villages, its majestic mountains and many lakes has become probably the best-known tourist region. Lower Bavaria, also called the granary of Bavaria, shows a glimpse of the Bavarian Forest behind its fertile, wide plateaus. The Upper Palatinate lures the visitor with its endless, untouched forests and gently rolling hills. Swabia with the Allgäu and its picture-book scenery invites the traveler to its magnificent mountain world. And, last but not least, although it was the last to become a part of Bavaria (in 1815), there is beautiful Franconia to enchant those who come to visit its romantic small towns and the meandering Main River sparkling in the proverbial Franconian sunshine as it winds its way among the vineyard-covered hills.

With their extraordinary wealth of architectural monuments the cities and towns of Bavaria represent every epoch of the German and European past. History comes alive at the sight of Regensburg or Augsburg, Würzburg or Nürnberg, Rothenburg ob der Tauber, Bamberg, Ansbach, Coburg or Passau, to mention only a few examples.

The accumulation of innumerable art treasures is not limited to the cities; there are more or less famous monasteries, places of pilgrimage, castles and palaces all over the countryside, most of them in lovely settings. The castles built by the unforgotten fairy-tale king, Ludwig II, are probably the best-known of them all.

The past of Bavaria is so extensive that it is taught in a university course all its own: *Bavarian History*.

It just happens to always have been and still is to this day a remarkable country,

this land of Bavaria.

A Few Words About the Bavarians

It is not possible to make a summary, general observation about the Bavarians: the people of Bavaria are as varied and different as are the various regions of the land they inhabit.

Shaped and marked by countryside, climate, and tribal origin, every tribe has to this day retained its own characteristics.

It is assumed that the *Old Bavarians* - the Altbaiern or Baiwarii a peasant tribe, immigrated from the East in the sixth century A.D., mixing with the few scattered Celts and Romans left in the land.

The future neighbors of this tribe were already here: the *Swabians* had settled the area between the Lech River and Lake Constance 300 years earlier. A branch of the tribe of the Alemanni, they had penetrated the country from the West.

The *Franconians*, on the other hand, are of west Germanic origin and are mentioned in documents dating back to the third century A.D. They came from the North-West and round off Bavaria to the North today.

What has become of all these tribes ?

Today, approximately 10 million people inhabit the regions mentioned above. A third of them live in towns and cities, while two-thirds live in rural regions and in the mountains. In the countryside, the people are mostly farmers, animal breeders and wine growers. Another major occupation is the maintanance of the large forests of Bavaria. In the towns and cities the Bavarians see to it that the good things of life are not destroyed by the haste and rush of modern age.

Foreigners often tend to regard the *Upper Bavarians*
as being the *Bavarians* in general.

No wonder: with their love of folk costumes, brass bands, beer
gardens and the "Oktoberfest", the *Upper Bavarians* are the most
conspicuous representatives of Bavaria.Rubbing shoulders with
large numbers of tourists has made the once-shy "Baiwarii" much
more self-assured.Thus, nowadays, they will often speak their
mind in a surprisingly frank manner.

True to their origin, the *Lower Bavarians* tend their highly prof-
itable land with diligence and devotion,often with the help of
verry modern technical equipment. The *Upper Palatines* and
Upper Franconians, border region dwellers in an often harsh
countryside,are not blessed quite so abundantly. Their ranks
supply a large quota of the workers in the spinning mills of
Upper Franconia. For many generations the unassuming people of
this region have, however,been famous far beyond the borders of
their land for their skill in the manufacture of glassware,
stoneware and china. The *Lower Franconians* in the towns and
cities are known as diplomats,because they do not say what they
think.Those of them who live in rural areas make their living
mainly by growing wine and sugar beets.As in the past, the
Central Franconians are famous for their industriousness and their
craftsmanship. And when we visit the *Swabians* in their examplary
little land,we realize that the people who live there are cir-
cumspect, efficient and reliable, who take good care of what they
have obtained through hard work.

All these tribes together have,throughout the centuries,enriched
the land of Bavaria with their diligence,craftsmanship and great
understanding of the arts.Their easygoing manner,with a tendency
to understatement,their helpfulness,their friendliness, their
sense of humor,their closeness to Nature and their deep-rooted
religiousness,maintained through every crisis, show us what they
are to this day,

these Bavarians.

Bavarian Cooking

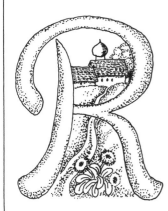egional Bavarian cooking should actually be divided into the original, peasant way of cooking, cooking in the private households of the Bavarian burghers, restaurant cooking, and the refined, gourmet way of cooking as practised, for example, at the court of the Kings of Bavaria where, according to ancient documents, rare, delicious, and complicated, time-consuming dishes were served, prepared after recipes obtained in part from Italy and France.

Long before the "Nouvelle Cuisine" wave the Bavarians had discovered sweetbreads and other organ meats as delicacies -- true, without exotic trimmings, but no less exquisite. The famous Crème Bavaroise (Bavarian Cream), which may be found on every international menu today, went to France first in order to return from there to Bavaria as the basis of every delicious and delicate Crème.

The aim of this book is to introduce Bavarian cooking as practised in private households, with recipes that are easy to follow for anyone who enjoys eating the natural way. -- The old recipes of our grandmothers managed to make do without adding any chemical agents -- which was probably the reason why everything tasted so good! In the recipes contained in this book this aspect has been preserved.

Bavarian cooking is dependent on first-class ingredients.There is
no room for cheating.The meat,which is mostly cooked in one large
piece, is clearly visible, nothing is "au gratin", cut in strips
and hidden under a thick sauce, or smothered with mayonnaise.
Bavarian cooking is not one of quick, pan-fried dishes and
grilled steaks; there are other masters in those culinary arts.
Here,the food is slowly cooked or simmered, whether it is meat
broth made on top of the stove or a roast cooked in the oven.
The seemingly longer-than-usual cooking time should not dis-
courage you. On the contrary! (See also p. 16) When the meat has
been tended to, you have time to prepare the accompanying dishes,
set the table, etc. There is no haste, no panic. The same goes
for a number of pastries which are prepared in the oven like,
for example, "Strudel" or yeast dumplings, "Rohrnudeln".

Today's private households have recognized that, with decreased
physical activity,brought about by the age of the car,the need
for concentrated fats as for example, lard and clarified butter
has diminished in Bavarian cooking. These fats are best substi-
tudet by a light vegetable or seed oil.Butter remains the favorite and most natural spread,however and cannot be banished entirely from Bavarian cooking.Unsalted butter, obtained from
sweet or sour cream, is used without exception.Since butter will
brown very quickly, a butter-and-oil mixture is used in certain
sautéed, roasted, or baked dishes, as indicated in the various
recipes.

In the case of old-time recipes calling for clarified butter it
is best to follow the recipe exactly to obtain the desired
taste: after all, these are not dishes you eat every day!

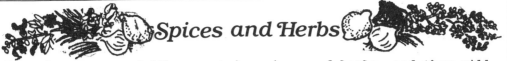

Spices and Herbs

Bavarians use, and like, certain spices and herbs, and they will not have their favorite dishes altered either by changing their taste or by adding, for example, fruit to meat dishes or onions to roast veal ... Ancient herbals, found above all in old Bavarian monasteries, prove the Bavarians' early interest in plants and herbs to enhance the taste of food and, in addition, to relieve or cure various ailments. Today, we profit from these experiences and realize that there are good reasons why Bavarian dishes are spiced in certain, specific ways.

Aniseed, Fennel, Coriander and *Caraway seed*, used in bread (which, in Bavaria, is mostly eaten freshly baked), have digestive and sedative qualities.

Caraway seed (Carum carvi L.) in bread, meat, and potato dishes, will activate gall function.

Chervil (Anthriscus crefolium) in soups, acts as a mild laxative.

Chives (Allium schoenaprasum) in soups and salads, act as a diuretic.

Garlic (Allium sativum L.) added to roast lamb or pork, is good for lowering blood pressure.

Horseradish (Cochlearia armoracia L.) eaten with meat, is good for the stomach and nerves.

Juniper berries (Juniperus communis L.) in game dishes, have germicidal qualities and a stimulative effect.

Lemon (Citrus medica) above all lemon rind, should be on hand at all times. Use only un-treated fruit, in sauces and pastry. Contains Vitamin C.

Lemon verbena (Melissa officinális L.) in salads, acts as a sedative and strengthens the nerves.

Lovage (Levisticum officinále Koch) in salads, soups, and hot pots, acts as a diuretic.

Marjoram (Majorana hortensis) in ground meat dishes, will strengthen the stomach.

Nutmeg strengthens the nerves.

Onion (Állium cepa) used raw or cooked, has an antibacterial effect.

Parsley (Petrosilium sativum): the smooth-leaved variety, favorite herb of the Bavarians, has blood-forming and diuretic qualities.

Parsnip, in soups and sauces, is a diuretic.

Savory (Satureia hortensis) added to beans and salads, is a stomachic.

Thyme (Thýmus vulgáris, L.) used in game dishes, acts as a disinfectant.

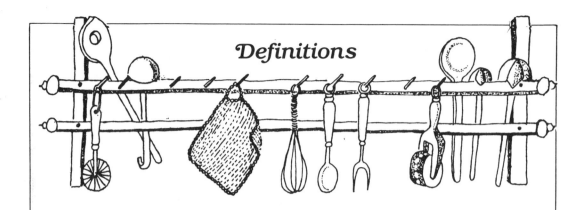

Definitions

Egg Whites, beaten: best results are obtained if using very cold and not too fresh egg whites, adding a pinch of salt or some lemon juice.

Flour: use finely ground wheat flour.

Foamy: when mixing butter to a foamy consistency, use soft butter, stir it first by itself, then gradually add the other ingredients.

Lemon: this is a favorite ingredient in Bavarian cooking.Only untreated fruit should be used, particularly if the recipe calls for the use of lemon peel or rind.

Mustard: the traditional Bavarian mustard, eaten with *Weisswurst* (White Sausage), is sweet and gets its dark color from the coarsely ground seeds. This kind, as well as a tangy, light-colored mustard, are important condiments for meat and sausages.

Noodles:in Bavaria, this definition not only covers the customary pasta strips; here, noodles may have quite different shapes and consist of widely varying ingredients.

Obstler is a fruit brandy.

Pepper: generally, black pepper is used.

Sautée: e.g., onions -- let them become glassy in hot fat; do not allow to brown.

Schwarzbrot: is a dark rye bread, baked mostly in round loaves, as opposed to the oblong loaves of *Mischbrot* (Mixed Bread).

Semmel: is the Bavarian name for a bun; in Northern Germany
a bun is called *Brötchen*.

Sift: let run through a sieve.

Simmer: slowly cook at low heat, do not boil.

Sour Cream in Bavaria has a thick consistency.

Vanilla Sugar and Vanillin Sugar are different products.
The recipes in this book call for Vanilla Sugar exclusively,
i.e., the scraped-out seeds of the vanilla bean, mixed with
sugar. Vanillin Sugar is a synthetic product.

Wammerl is streaky bacon; plain or smoked, it is used often
in Bavarian cooking.

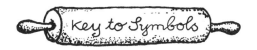

Key to Symbols

*   prepare ahead

Tbs level tablespoon

tsp level teaspoon

oz. ounce(s)

qt quart = 4 cups

lb pound

in. inch

The recipes will serve 4 persons unless indicated otherwise.

Unsalted butter and vegetable oil were used throughout the
book. No olive oil is used in Bavarian cooking.

The American-Bavarian Kitchen Stove

During the War of Independence,an American physicist by the name of Benjamin Thompson left his home country for England. In 1784 he entered into the service of the State of Bavaria,reorganizing its army.His work included setting up the large kitchen of the Military Academy in Munich. Noting that the cook had the daily task of preparing a roast for 200 persons on an open fire,he hit upon an ingenious idea: he constructed a cooking stove with a closed oven. It was soon realized that meat cooked in this oven tasted better,was much more wholesome,and lost less of its weight than meat roasted on a spit. And, as an added benefit, considerably less wood was needed for this cooking process.The further development of Mr. Thompson's cooking stove,with an iron cooking surface,water container,and removable rings,turned out to be a blessing for the less-than-affluent as,apart from all its other advantages, it also provided them with a heated room. - In his book "Kleine Schriften" ("Little Writings"), published in

1803, this man of many talents describes exactly his designs for pots and pans.But,as if this were not enough,he also constructed the first steam cooker (see drawing). And then he devised a recipe for preparing meat broth the right way,as we make it today,i.e.,to set the meat on the stove in a pot of cold water if we want the soup to be really good.If the emphasis is on juicy meat,it is to be placed into hot or boiling broth.

For his great merits in various - to a large extent social - areas,Benjamin Thompson was awarded the title of Count Rumford.

His motto was:

> Happy shall I be if the knowledge
> of having lived for a good purpose
> accompanies me to my grave.

Unsere Mütter und
Großmütter kochten
auf solchen Herden.

Our mothers and
our grandmothers
cooked on this
kind of stove.

Beer

Bavaria and beer are mentioned mostly in one breath, and not with- out some justification. Bavaria can look back upon an old beer brewing tradition. Afterall, the oldest brewery, Weihenstephan near Munich, has been there since the year 1040. Every third brewery in the world is located on Bavarian soil.

The quality of beer has been determined, to a large extent, since 1516, when William IV., Duke of Bavaria, issued his edict regulat- ing the degree of beer purity. It decrees that beer may be pro- duced from 4 ingredients only:

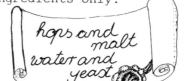

hops and malt
water and yeast

This edict has remained in force to this day and is subject to strict control.

Thus it is no wonder that Bavarian beer tastes so good!

The choice of beers is so great that it is impossible to list every individual brewery by name. For example, in the lakeside town of Starnberg as well as in Munich there are restaurants selling 101 different kinds of beer! Whether you choose to drink a Märzenbier, a Starkbier, a light Helles, a Champagner-Weisse, a Hefeweissbier, a light or dark Bock, an Altbier or a Rauchbier -- your Bavarian beer will always give you full satisfaction.

Beer temperatures are a matter of taste, but beer that is too warm will make you tired. In Bavaria, beer is drunk at approx. 45° F -- abroad, it is frequently served at a colder temperature.

Note: Bottled Weissbier should never be shaken or jolted in any way before being opened. If you like your Weissbier with a slice of lemon, use untreated fruit, otherwise the froth will collapse. This is also the reason why a Bavarian will get grumpy if some- one wearing lipstick drinks from his glass, chasing away the lovely head of his beer.

Wine

Wine from Bavaria is not as well known by far as is beer – unless, of course, we speak of Frankenwein (Franconian Wine) specifically, which, filled into its specially shaped *Bocksbeutel* (Buck's Bag) bottles, is highly regarded far beyond the borders of the country, particularly by real connoisseurs of wine.

The special Bocksbeutel bottle may be used only for Franconian wines and for the so-called Mauerweine (Wall Wines) from Baden, which come from a former Franconian territory.

Frankenwein was the favorite wine of the poet Goethe; it counts as a "gentleman's wine and should be drunk to philosophize, not to get grossly drunk on.

The three largest vineyards of Germany are in the Würzburg region. The oldest vineyard, the Bürgerspital, has been cultivated since 1319, the Juliusspital since 1576, followed by the Hofkellerei.

Fermenting grape juice – sometimes still a little warm and milky white – is served under the name of *Federweisser*. Often it is just a matter of hours during which it has that incomparable effervescence – until it collapses to become Most (cider). If a person drinks too much of it, he or she will also collapse – invariably toppling over backward, a phenomenon that remains unsolved.

"Most" Cider

Most will also be found in fruit-growing regions, where it is made of apples, often mixed with pears to make it milder. The peasants used to drink it, taking it along to the fields and mixing it with water. Most mixed with effervescent mineral water is very refreshing.

Radlermass

First pour 2 cups lemonade into a 1 L beer mug. Add 2 cups well cooled light beer. Use a clear sparkling lemonade, not a fruit juice!

This is the thing to drink on hot summer days or after a mountain climbing tour.

Russenmass

Like the Radlermass, the "Russ", as the Bavarians have fondly nicknamed this drink, will quench your thirst efficiently and has less alcohol than beer.

2 cups Weissbier ("White Beer")
2 cups lemonade

First pour a clear lemonade into a 1 L beer mug and add slowly a well cooled beer. Use a clear, sparkling lemonade, not a fruit juice!

Spezi

This is an American-Bavarian mixture that has nicely taken root in Bavaria. It is a combination of Coca-Cola and lemonade, served with an ice cube and a slice of lemon on top.

Schorle

"Schorle" is drunk mostly in the Franconian and Swabian wine regions. It is generally prepared with a dry white wine, but sometimes a red wine is preferred. The mixture varies from one pub to the next:

1/3 wine	2/3 mineral water or soda
1/2 wine	1/2 mineral water or soda

The drink should be very cool. Sometimes an ice cube and a slice of lemon is added, but that is not traditional.

in memoriam
Pepperl

Gschwemm

People get thirsty in a bakery, and beer is not always the answer. That is why "Gschwemm" was invented. It can only be prepared if you have access to a very cool cellar.

2 1/2 gallons water
1 oz. yeast
1 1/2 lbs sugar
1 small bouquet
woodruff or
2 lbs raspberries
    or
2 lbs strawberries

In a large stone crock, crumble the yeast into the water, add the sugar, and mix well. Add the woodruff, or the raspberries, or the strawberries, mix, and let stand, covered, for 2 weeks. Strain off and fill into clean bottles. Seal the bottles with corks. In a week you have a slightly effervescent, refreshing fruit drink.

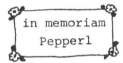

Oberstdorf Ski-Water

This drink was served in earlier times in the ski châlet of Nebelhorn Mountain. Whether served hot in the winter or cold in the summer, you will always enjoy it. It is a natural, good drink which will frequently quench your thirst better than a sweet lemonade. For one drink, take:
2 Tbs freshly pressed lemon juice, 1-3 Tbs raspberry syrup, depending on its sugar content. Add boiling water. In the summer, add cold, effervescent mineral water.

Brotzeit and Vesper Menu

1 pair Weisswürste (white Bavarian sausages)
  with sweet mustard and pretzels
4 Nürnberg Schweinsbratwürstel
  (fried pork sausages) with Sauerkraut
2 Regensburg sausages with hot mustard
  and Kipferl (crescent bun)
2 Knackwürste
  (a thick meat sausage) in vinegar and oil
Wurstsalat (sausage salad) made from Nürnberg
  Stadtwurst (a coarse pork sausage)
Tölzer Gselchtes
  (smoked meat from the town
  of Bad Tölz) with bread
Franconian Gelegter (a fine-grain head cheese)
  with Landbrot (country bread)
White or red Pressack (head cheese) with bread
White or red Pressack in vinegar and oil
Beef in vinegar and oil
Franconian Häckerbrotzeit (wine-grower's snack):
  boiled, smoked pork ribs, smoked Leberwurst
  (liver sausage) and smoked"Knäudele"
  (black pudding)
Iphöfer Wengerts Vesper (Iphof Vineyard snack):
  smoked sausages as above, smoked meat, and plum brandy
Tellersulz, Bratensulz, Knöcherlsulz
  (boiled pork jelly, roast meat jelly, knuckle jelly)
Swabian Hirschgeräuchertes (smoked deer meat)
Swiss cheese from the Allgäu region with butter,
  bread, and a small glass of Obstler (fruit brandy)
Spiced and herbed Camembert or Obatzter
White radishes with bread, butter and chives

Tellerfleisch (Munich boiled beef)
Kronfleisch (boiled beef)
Milzwurst (milt sausage) in broth
Calf's lungs with Knödel (dumpling)
Veal kidneys, sautéed or sour
Calf's liver, sautéed or sour
Sweetbread, sour
Blaue Zipfel (Franconian sausages)
Calf's or Pork's tongue, sour

  Home-made hot Leberkäse

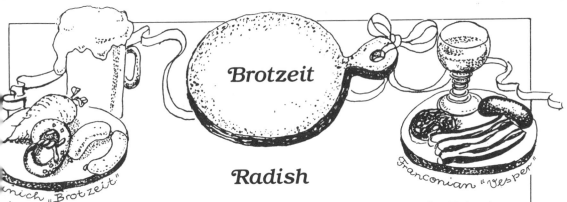

Brotzeit

Munich „Brotzeit"

Franconian „Vesper"

Radish

The best-known Bavarian radish is called "Munich Beer". This is
a thick, white kind, which has to be sliced the right way, of
course: this is done by hand, lengthwise, as it will taste quite
differently if cut with a radish slicer which cut the slices
into spirals. Radishes should not be salted too generously, as
the salt will flush out all digestive components. In the old days
radishes were salted and allowed to "cry" for a long time; the
result was a heavy stomach and gas. Prepare radishes in the
following manner:

Cut off the greens, shave off the small roots but leave on the
"tail" so you have something to hold the radish by. Cut the radishes lengthwise into thin slices, but not quite all the way
through or the "leaves" will fall apart. Salt the radishes
lightly and let them draw briefly. Gourmets will put a flake of
butter on each slice, roll up the slice and pop it in their
mouths.

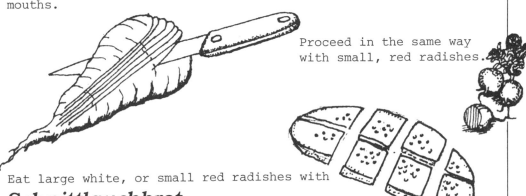

Proceed in the same way
with small, red radishes.

Eat large white, or small red radishes with

Schnittlauchbrot

Spread a slice of dark bread (Schwarzbrot) evenly with butter,
sprinkle generously with chopped chives and some salt, and cut
it up into small "Häuserl".

Weißwürste

"Weisswürste", the typical Bavarian "white sausages", will never taste as good at home as they do in a beer hall. They should be eaten with sweet mustard and a fresh brown bread bun (called a "Römische") or a Bavarian pretzel ("Bretzn").For a party at home or at a Bavarian buffet, Weisswürste are a welcome dish, and are to be prepared as follows:

Place the Weisswürste loosely into a large pot with plenty of cold water and heat the water until small bubbles form at the bottom of the pot. Take the pot from the heat immediately and let the sausages draw approx. 20 minutes. Weisswürste should never be allowed to boil, as they will burst if overheated.

Leberkäs

"Leberkäse" translates into "liver cheese", but it is actually a meatloaf-type dish containing neither liver nor cheese.It should probably be called "life cheese", as it has always had the capacity to bring tired, hungry people back to life. In Franconia, by the way,it is prepared partly with liver.To make Leberkäse at home would be a wasted effort,since a regular kitchen is not equipped to prepare the meat with the method used by butchers (who chop it up together with ice cubes to a special consistency). It is best to buy Leberkäse fresh and hot at the butcher's.

Bratwürste

"Bratwürste" or fried sausages come in many varieties. The sausages made in the Franconian towns of Ochsenfurt and Coburg are larger than the famous "Rostbratwürstle" of Nürnberg and Regensburg, which are no longer than your little finger. These small ones will only taste right in the atmosphere of their local Wurst kitchens. The large, Franconian sausages, and the regular medium-sized pork Bratwürste may be pan-fried or grilled, using the following method: let the sausages draw briefly in hot water, dip them into milk, and brown them on all sides in their own juice (do not use any additional oil or fat).

Franconian Sausage, Sour

"Blaue Zipfel" will appear on every restaurant menu in the Würzburg area and in the small villages along the Main River. If you are able to obtain good quality, coarse pork sausages (the large size, not the small grilling sausages), you will have no trouble preparing the "Blaue Zipfel" yourself. The following recipe is for 4 persons.

1 basic recipe "Blausud", p. 56
1 large onion, sliced
4 pairs fresh pork sausages
   ("Bratwürste")

Add the sliced onion to the basic "Blausud" recipe in a heatproof pot. After the liquid has boiled, lower the heat and place the sausages into the hot but no longer boiling liquid. Simmer slowly for 15-25 minutes and serve in the cooking liquid.

Grilled Regensburg Sausages

You may use a grill or a frying pan for grilling the sausages. Count 2 Regensburg sausages "Knack-würste" per person. Leave on the skins, making small, slanting incisions on both sides of the sausages. Using no shortening, grill the sausages, turning them constant-ly. Serve with dark bread and sweet mustard. Great for open-air picnics!

Regensburg Sausage Salad

For 1 person:
2 Regensburg
   Meat Sausages
   ("Knackwürste")
onion rings, to taste
vinegar mixed with
   water, to taste
oil, to taste

Remove the thin skin from the sausages and cut them into thin slices. Arrange the sausage slices on a plate in a tile pattern. Distribute the onion rings evenly over the sausage slices. Pour the watered vinegar and oil over the sausage slices and serve.

Boiled Beef Salad

If you have any leftover boiled beef, you may want to use it in the following salad:

approx. 1/2 lb boiled beef
1 small onion, sliced
1 apple
2 Tbs vinegar
beef stock (with all fat removed)
2 Tbs oil
chives, chopped

Cut the beef in small slices or strips, and, in a bowl, mix it with the onion rings. Add the peeled, cored, and slivered apple (optional). Thin the vinegar with the beef stock to taste, pour the mixture over the meat, mix and let draw for 10 minutes. Add the oil, mix again, and sprinkle with the chives.

Makes an excellent summer dish. Also very good for breakfast "the morning after."

Spiced Cheese   "Obatzter"

2 oz. butter
3 Tbs thick cream
3 1/2 oz. ripe Camembert cheese
1 small onion, finely chopped
dash of pepper
1 Tbs sweet paprika powder

In a bowl, mix the butter, cream, and Camembert, using a fork or the kneading attachment of your mixer to mash up the cheese. Add the chopped onion, a dash of freshly ground pepper, and the paprika, and mix well. -- For variety you may wish to prepare this mixture using 3 1/2 oz. cream cheese (Gervais) or, if you prefer a stronger taste, Limburger cheese.

Unterdürrbach "Caviar"

This is a Franconian relative of the Spiced Cheese ("Obatzter"), above.

1/4 lb Limburger -or- Romadur cheese
1 1/2 oz. butter
1 onion, chopped
1 Tbs sweet paprika powder
1 Tbs caraway seeds

Remove the rind of the cheese and mash it up with the aid of a fork or the kneading attachment of your mixer. Mix well with butter, onion, paprika and caraway seeds. Arrange in a mound on a wooden plate, surround it with small pickled gherkins and serve with dark bread. A nice Franconian wine, or a so-called "Federweisser" (a white wine from Swabia or Franconia) goes well with this "caviar."

Soups

Meat Broth

1 large yellow onion
1 Tbs oil
1 lb beef bones
1-2 marrow bones
1-2 lbs boiling beef

up to 12 cups water
2 Tbs salt
1 small piece ea.
beef liver,milt,
and heart
2 carrots
1/2 celery root
1 leek
2 parsnips
1 sprig celery
1 sprig lovage

Cut the unpeeled onion in half.In a large (5 qts.) pot, brown the onion halves in the oil,to lend the soup a nice,golden color.Add the bones and meat (short loin, brisket,flat shoulder,or round),and the water.

Then add the salt, liver, milt and heart as well as

the vegetables, cut into pieces

Bring everything to a boil, reduce the heat,and let the soup simmer for 1 1/4-2 hours (approx.1/2 hour in a pressure cooker). If the meat is of primary importance, it should be put into the pot when the water is already boiling (see Boiled Beef and Munich Boiled Beef p.60). Meat Broth keeps well in the freezer.

IMPORTANT: In the summer, cook the broth without salt, as the soup will turn sour more rapidly if salted.

Swabian "Flädle" Soup

6 1/2 oz. flour
2 eggs
pinch of salt
1/2 cup sparkling
mineral water
a small amount of
frying fat
or oil
6 cups meat broth

Mix the flour, eggs and salt until smooth and let stand for about 1/2 hour. In a pan, bake flat, round pancakes (Flädle), tilting the pan when pouring in the dough to coat the bottom of the pan thinly.
Cut into strips and serve in hot meat broth.

"Brätstrudel" Soup

6 1/2 oz."Kalbsbrät"
(professionally prepared
ground veal)
4 Tbs heavy cream
1 Tbs parsley, chopped
1/2 lemon, untreated
1/4 tsp thyme
pinch of nutmeg,
ground
6 cups meat broth

Prepare Swabian Flädle as described above. In a bowl, mix well the Kalbsbrät, heavy cream, parsley, grated lemon rind, thyme and nutmeg. Spread in a 1 in. layer on the Flädle, roll them up and let stand for 15 minutes, then cut them up to 1 1/2 in. bits, place them carefully into the simmering broth and let them draw 5 minutes.

Ham Dumpling Soup

Serves 4-6 persons

Prepare 1/2 basic recipe for "Semmelknödel" (p.112), adding an extra 6 1/2 oz. raw ham, finely chopped.
Form small (1 in.dia.) dumplings, and let them simmer 10 - 12 minutes in 7 cups meat broth. Serve sprinkled with chopped chives.

Pastry Patch Soup

Serves 6 persons

Prepare 1/2 basic recipe of noodle dough (p. 115). Cut the rolled-out dough into 1/2-3/4 in. squares and simmer them 6-8 minutes in 8 cups broth. (Or break ready-made broad, flat noodles into square bits.) Season the soup well and serve sprinkled with chopped chives.

from cham

Swabian Wedding Soup

Serves 8 persons

Swabian Wedding Soup consists of a very good meat broth, garnished with the following:

Liver Dumplings:
1/2 recipe, (p. 33)

"Brät" Dumplings:
7 oz."Kalbsbrät"
1 egg
approx. 1 Tbs
ice-cold milk
1 Tbs flour
1/2 lemon, untreated
1 Tbs parsley, chopped

(Kalbsbrät is professionally prepared ground veal)

Mix the "Kalbsbrät", egg, milk, and flour well. Add the grated lemon rind and chopped parsley. Using a teaspoon, cut small button-shaped pieces and let them draw in the simmering broth 5 minutes.

Fried "Spätzle":
1/2 recipe
puff pastry, (p. 156)
frying fat

Prepare the puff pastry. Heat the fat in a pan, drip in the dough through a Spätzle sieve, fry the Spätzle until golden yellow, and drain well.

approx. 8 cups
hot meat broth
chives, chopped

Serve all the above garnishings together in the hot meat broth, sprinkled with chopped chives.

"Brät" Button Soup

from Caroline Schram

Prepare Brät Dumplings as described above. (This quantity will serve 4.) Add to 5 cups simmering meat broth and let draw 5 minutes. This is also a very good addition to Flädle Soup.

Meat Pouch Soup

Prepare Meat Pouches (p. 116). (This quantity will serve 4.) Add to 5 cups simmering meat broth and let draw 5 minutes.

Egg Drop Soup

5 cups meat broth
1 large egg
1 Tbs flour
salt to taste
nutmeg, ground,
to taste
chives, chopped

Bring the broth to a boil. In a cup, mix all ingredients well. Pour into the boiling soup in a thin stream. As soon as the last of the egg mixture has been added to the boiling soup, the soup is ready. Serve sprinkled with chives.

Stritzel Soup

Prepare "Stritzel" following the recipe on p. 110. Thinly cut up 1 Stritzel per person. Arrange the bits in individual serving bowls, pour boiling meat broth over them, let them draw briefly, and serve sprinkled with chives.

Barley Soup

6 Tbs pearl barley
5 cups meat or bone broth
1 Tbs vinegar
1 egg
chives, chopped
parsley, chopped

Wash the barley in lukewarm water. Bring the broth to a boil, season to taste, and add the barley. Simmer slowly for 3/4 hour. Season with vinegar to taste. Optional: thicken with an egg, lightly beaten. Sprinkle with chives and parsley before serving.
This soup is said to cure an upset stomach.

from Augsburg

Cheese Diamonds Soup

2 Tbs butter
2 egg yolks
3 Tbs flour
3 Tbs grated Swiss cheese
2 egg whites

Mix the butter and egg yolks vigorously until foamy, add the flour and grated cheese, and mix well. Fold in the stiffly beaten egg whites. In a well-buttered small roasting pan or heatproof dish, bake the mixture (it should reach approx. 1/2 inch high in the dish) until golden yellow. Cut it in diamond-shaped pieces and serve in hot meat broth.

Rumford Soup

Sir Benjamin Thompson, Count Rumford, "invented" this soup, thereby contributing to the well-being of the army and the poorer strata of the population with a nutritious, healthy, and cheap dish.

1/4 lb dried yellow
peas
1 large onion, chopped
4 Tbs pearl barley
1 1/2 oz. bacon, diced
1 1/2 cups bone broth
2 large potatoes, diced

Serves
5
persons

Soak the peas overnight in 2 qts water. Next day, add the chopped onion to the peas, cook until the peas are tender, and pass the mixture through a sieve. In a large pot, slowly fry the diced bacon until the fat has melted, add the barley, stir, add the broth, and let simmer 20 minutes. Meanwhile, peel and dice the potatoes and add them to the barley mixture. When they are done, add the pea soup, mix well, and season to taste. This is quite a hearty soup!

Toasted Semolina Soup (Old Bavarian recipe)

1 oz. butter or oil
2 1/2 oz. coarse semolina
5 cups meat or bone stock
1/2 tsp salt (if needed)

In a large saucepan, heat the butter or oil. Add the semolina, and toast to a golden color. Slowly add the meat or bone stock (and the salt if the stock is unsalted). Cover (if uncovered, the soup will develop a film on top), bring to a boil, and let simmer for 15-20 minutes, stirring a few times.

1 egg
parsley, chopped

In a bowl, beat the egg together with a few spoonfuls of soup and return to the saucepan. Mix well. Serve sprinkled with parsley.

Bone Stock

Bone stock is prepared in the same way as meat broth (p. 27), but using 2 lbs beef bones in place of the meat. Veal bones will make the stock cloudy and therefore suitable as a base for "bound" soups only.

Bread Soup   (Lower Bavarian recipe)

approx. 1/4 lb
  stale brown bread
1 qt bone stock, spiced
1 onion, sliced
2 Tbs shortening
chives, chopped
parsley, chopped

Use the crusty end of the bread for best results. Cut the bread in thin slices, place into a pre-heated soup bowl and douse with the boiling hot bone stock that has already been spiced to taste. In a saucepan, brown the onion rings in the shortening and distribute over the soup. Sprinkle with chives and parsley and serve immediately.

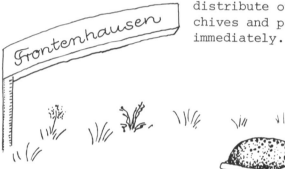

Stewed Bread Soup

approx. 1/4 lb leftover
  stale brown bread
1 oz. shortening
1 onion, coarsely chopped
1 carrot, diced
1 qt bone stock
salt and pepper
  to taste
1 tsp vinegar
1 egg (Optional)

In a large saucepan, toast the bread, onion and carrot in the shortening. Add the bone stock, bring to a boil and simmer for 1/2 hour. Pass the soup through a sieve and add salt, pepper and vinegar, to taste.
If you want to improve the soup, beat the egg in a small bowl with a few spoonfuls of the soup, return the mixture to the saucepan and mix well.

Liver Dumpling Soup

10 stale white buns or
1 lb stale white bread
1 1/2 cup boiling milk
3/4 lb beef liver
1 Tbs marjoram
1/4 tsp pepper
1 tsp salt
1 onion, finely
chopped
1 1/2 oz. butter
2 Tbs parsley,
chopped
1 lemon (untreated)
3 whole eggs
approx. 10 cups
meat broth
chives, chopped

Slice up the buns or bread very thinly, douse with the hot milk and let stand, covered, for 1 hour. Wash the liver, shred it with the back of a knife or grind it, and add it to the soaked bread. In a small pan heat up the marjoram (heat enhances its taste) and add it to the mixture, together with the salt and pepper. Fry the onion in the butter until glassy, and add to it the grated lemon rind and chopped parsley. Mix all with the meat mixture. Shape the dough into dumplings of approx. 3 in. dia., and simmer the dumplings in boiling meat broth for 20 minutes. Serve in the broth, sprinkled with parsley, or serve the drained dumplings with Sauerkraut. A black radish, grated very finely, tastes delicious with liver dumplings and boiled beef.

"Lebernockerl" Soup

3 1/2 oz. beef liver
2 oz. butter
4 Tbs flour
1 egg
1/2 Tbs marjoram
salt, pepper
1 Tbs parsley,
chopped
1 Tbs onions,
chopped
1/2 lemon (untreated)
6 cups meat broth
chives, chopped

Shred the liver with the back of a knife. Stir the butter until foamy, mix in the flour, add the egg and the liver. In a small pan, heat up the marjoram, and mix with the liver, salt, pepper, parsley, onion and grated lemon rind. Using 2 teaspoons, form a test "Nockerl" and simmer it in the boiling broth. If it remains firm, form the dough into "Nockerl" and let them simmer 5-7 minutes. (If necessary, some flour may be added to the dough.) Serve the soup sprinkled with chives.

Liver "Spätzle" Soup

Drip the Liver Nockerl dough (p. 33), through the holes of a "Spätzle" sieve into boiling meat broth, stir, let draw no longer than 2-3 minutes, and serve.

Grated Dough Soup   Serves 5-6 persons

1/4 lb flour
1 small egg
1/4 tsp salt
2 qts meat broth
chives, chopped, or
parsley, chopped

On a pastry board, knead the flour, egg and salt to a firm dough. Grate the dough coarsely, and spread the gratings on the board to dry. Then let the gratings simmer approx. 10 minutes in the boiling broth. Serve sprinkled with parsley or chives.

Swabian Crumble Soup   Serves 5-6 persons

1/4 lb flour
1 small egg
salt
1 eggshell-full
of water

Sift the flour onto a pastry board, lightly beat the egg with the salt and water, pour the mixture over the flour and loosen it with a fork. Rub it between your hands to loose crumbs, let the crumbs dry briefly, then simmer them in boiling meat broth 8-10 minutes.

Semolina "Nockerl" Soup

1 1/2 oz. butter
2 oz. coarse semolina
1 egg
salt and ground
nutmeg
8 cups meat broth,
seasoned to taste
chives, chopped

Stir the butter vigorously until foamy, gradually add the semolina alternating with the egg. Season with salt and ground nutmeg. Let the dough stand 1/2 hour. Using 2 teaspoons, form small Nockerl and drop them in the boiling broth. Reduce the heat and simmer the Nockerl approx. 1/2 hour. Serve the soup sprinkled with chopped chives. Semolina Nockerl may be deep-frozen.

Creamed Asparagus Soup

This soup may be prepared from either the water saved from cooked asparagus, or thin asparagus spears.

3/4-1lb asparagus spears
2 Tbs butter
1 Tbs vegetable oil
2 Tbs flour
1/2 cup cold milk approx.
4 cups asparagus liquid
1 egg yolk
2 Tbs sweet cream
1/2 tsp lemon juice
chives,chopped
 - or -
parsley,chopped

Peel the asparagus spears and cut them into 1 in. bits.Boil them for approx.20 minutes. In a 2 qt.saucepan,melt butter and heat with oil.Stir in the flour,add the milk and stir until smooth.Add the asparagus liquid,a little at a time.Bring to a boil, and simmer for at least 15 minutes to remove the floury taste.Add the asparagus bits.

In a small bowl,mix the egg yolk,cream and lemon juice.Add a few spoonfuls of soup, mix,and return the mixture to the saucepan. Serve with chives or parsley.If you use only asparagus water without asparagus bits,serve the soup with croûtons (diced white bread toasted in butter).

Herb Soup
Kräutlsuppe

When Bavarians speak of Kräutl,they will be thinking first and foremost of chervil (Anthriscus crefolium) which may be bought in almost any Bavarian market.A Kräutlsuppe or herb soup can also be prepared with spinach and various wild herbs like watercress,sorrel,dandelion,and pimpernel.Traditionally,a Kräutlsuppe will be served in Bavaria on Easter (Maundy) Thursday, called Gründonnerstag (Green Thursday).

1/2 lb herbs
1 onion,finely chopped
3 Tbs oil
2 Tbs flour
5 cups broth (meat,bone,or vegetable)
1/4 tsp salt
2 stale buns
butter to fry

Wash the herbs in salted water,remove thick stalks,and finely chop the leaves. In a saucepan,cook the onions briefly in oil until glassy,add flour,and mix only slightly. Add 2 cups broth,stirring to dissolve any lumps and let boil for 15 minutes. Then add the herbs and the remainder of the broth an bring briefly to a boil. Season with salt.To serve: thinly slice 2 stale buns, toast them in butter until crisp and golden, and top the soup with the fried bun slices.

Chicken Noodle Soup

1/2 lb boiling beef
1 boiling chicken,
whole

Prepare meat broth (p. 27), using only
1/2 lb beef and no marrow bone. Add the
cleaned chicken, gizzard and heart to
the boiling broth, return to the boil,
cover, and simmer 1 1/2-2 hours, until
tender (approx. 1/2 hour in a pressure
cooker, but conventional way is preferred, to avoid overcooking). Drain
and put the chicken in a warm place,
covered, to rest briefly. Strain the
broth.

1 lb flat noodles
(1/5 in.wide)
parsley, chopped
chives, chopped

As a main dish for 4 persons:
Prepare noodles (p. 115), or use ready-
made noodles. Cook in boiling salted
water approx. 6-8 minutes. Do not overcook! Chill with cold water and add to
the chicken broth (cooking the noodles
in the broth itself will make it
cloudy).
Remove bones and skin, cut the meat
into 1-in. squares, return it to the
broth and correct the seasoning. Serve
sprinkled generously with fresh parsley
and chives.

Marrow Dumpling Soup

2 large marrow bones
(approx. 2 oz. marrow)
1 oz. butter
1 egg
salt
2 Tbs flour
2 Tbs stale bred
crumbs
6 cups meat broth
parsley, chopped

Shake the hot, cooked marrow from the
bones into a pan, strain into a bowl,
and let cool. Add the butter, and mix
until fluffy. Mix in the egg and salt
to taste, add the flour and breadcrumbs,
and mix well. Let the dough draw briefly, then form cherry-sized balls and
simmer them in seasoned broth 12 minutes. Serve soup sprinkled with parsley.

Milt Sausage

Milt sausage is an old Bavarian specialty. We differentiate between Lower Bavarian milt sausage, mainly served in soup, and the Upper Bavarian variety, called "Browned Milt Sausage".

1 calf's caul
(great omentum)
1 calf's brain
1 sweetbread
1/4-1/2 lb calf's liver
1/2-3/4 lb veal
4 Tbs parsley, chopped
4 Tbs onions, chopped
peel of 1 lemon,
untreated, chopped
salt & pepper to taste

1 large calf's milt

Wash the calf's caul well and spread to dry. Boil the sweetbread briefly. Remove the filaments from sweetbread and brain. Dice the brain, sweetbread and veal, cut the liver in strips, and arrange each type of meat separately on a platter. Mix the parsley, onion and lemon peel. Fill the caul, arranging on it lengthwise a row ea. of the various meats. Season evenly with salt, pepper, and the herb mixture. Cut off any thick edges. Fold in the ends and roll up the caul. (Size of roll should fit the milt).

Choose an undamaged milt. Cut off one end. Using a long knife, cut a deep pocket into the milt, almost all the way through. Pull the milt over the caul roll until it is completely surrounded. Tie the cut end with a thick string (thin thread will cut the milt!).

meat broth
chives chopped

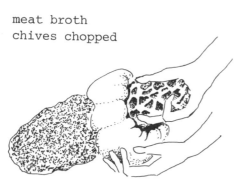

In a large pot, bring the strained and seasoned meat broth to a boil, add the milt sausage, and simmer 1 hour. Let rest approx. 10 mins., then cut into 1 in. slices. Place the slices into soup bowls, pour hot broth over them and sprinkle with chopped chives. Very good!

Recipe: Grandma Obner

Milt Sausage

Prepare 1 calf's caul,1 calf's milt,as well as 1 calf's brain,
1 sweetbread,and 1/4-1/2 lb calf's liver as described in the recipe for Lower Bavarian Milt Sausage (p.38), leaving off the
veal.Prepare the parsley,onion and lemon peel following the
same recipe.

1/2-3/4 lb profes-
sionally prepared
ground veal "Kalbsbrät"
salt & pepper to taste
meat broth

Mix the diced meats with the Kalbsbrät
(which you get at the butcher's),add
the greens,and season with salt and pep-
per.Stuff the prepared milt with the
meat mixture,and roll the stuffed milt
into the caul.Tie up this package well
in the same way as you do with a rolled
roast,and let it simmer gently in the
meat broth for approx.1 hour.

Lift the roll from the broth and let it rest approx.10 minutes
before slicing.Cut into 1/2 in.slices and fry the slices in
butter,or coat the slices with flour,egg wash,and stale bread
crumbs in that order and fry them a golden brown.Serve with a
mixed salad.This recipe is easier to prepare than the Lower
Bavarian variety -- but, then, that one is something very
special.

Milt Snack Soup

3 buns (yesterday's)
5 oz. beef's milt
1 small onion,
chopped
peel of 1/2 lemon
(untreated),finely
chopped
2 Tbs parsley
1/2 tsp marjoram,minced
salt & pepper to taste
1 egg
oil to fry
5 cups meat broth,
seasoned to taste
chives,chopped

Cut the buns into 1/5 in.slices.Wash
and scrape out the milt,using a table-
spoon.Add the onion,lemon peel,parsley,
and marjoram,and season with salt and
freshly ground pepper to taste.Add the
egg, mix everything well,and spread the
mixture on the bun slices.In a frying
pan,heat the oil and fry the bun slices
on both sides,beginning with the side
spread with the milt mixture.Heat up
the meat broth.Distribute the milt
snacks in soup plates,pour the broth
over them,and sprinkle with chopped
chives.

Fine Potato Soup

This soup, followed by a substantial pastry,
is a favorite meal of many Bavarians.

1 oz.dried mushrooms
(optional)
1 lb potatoes
2 carrots
1/4 celery root
1 parsnip
1 large onion
2 Tbs oil
5 cups broth or
water
salt,pepper,marjoram,
lemon rind (untreated),
lovage,parsley,
celery leaves
basil leaves

Soak the mushrooms in lukewarm water.
Peel and wash the potatoes and cut
them in 1 in.cubes,together with the
carrots and celery root.Finely cut up
the parsnip.Chop the onion and sauté
it in the oil in a deep pot until
light yellow.Add the vegetables,mix,
add the broth or water,and simmer for
30 minutes.10 minutes before the end
of cooking time,add the drained and
pressed-out mushrooms.Season the soup
with salt,pepper,and the finely
chopped herbs.If the soup is too
thick,add some more broth.Optional:
add 1 Tbs sour cream.

Franconian Potato Soup

Prepare as described above,but cook a
piece of dark bread rind along with
the potatoes,leave off the mushrooms,
and season only with salt,pepper,and
marjoram.

Potato Soup with Bacon

Prepare Fine Potato Soup as described
above,leaving off all seasonings
except salt,pepper,and marjoram.
Dice 2 1/2 oz.smoked streaky bacon,
fry it,and top the soup with the
bacon and hot bacon fat before
serving.

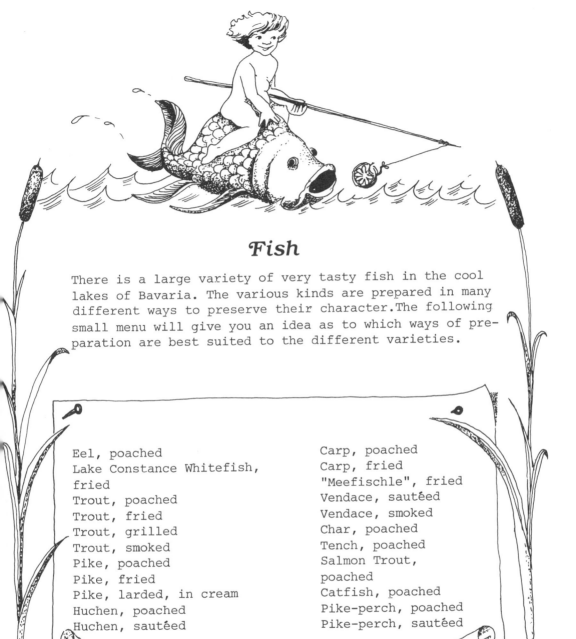

Fish

There is a large variety of very tasty fish in the cool lakes of Bavaria. The various kinds are prepared in many different ways to preserve their character. The following small menu will give you an idea as to which ways of preparation are best suited to the different varieties.

Eel, poached
Lake Constance Whitefish, fried
Trout, poached
Trout, fried
Trout, grilled
Trout, smoked
Pike, poached
Pike, fried
Pike, larded, in cream
Huchen, poached
Huchen, sautéed

Carp, poached
Carp, fried
"Meefischle", fried
Vendace, sautéed
Vendace, smoked
Char, poached
Tench, poached
Salmon Trout, poached
Catfish, poached
Pike-perch, poached
Pike-perch, sautéed

Regensburg Fish Sausages
Crayfish in Broth

Crayfish

Crayfish should be quite fresh and alive. Brush them thoroughly under running cold water. Fill a large pot with plenty of salted water, add 1 Tbs caraway seeds and 1 lemon slice. Bring the water to a boil and add the crayfish, head first, so they are killed instantly. If the tails are crooked, the crayfish are fresh. Let the crayfish boil for 1/4 hour, then take them from the heat and let them draw in the broth. Preheat a large, covered soup tureen, transfer the crayfish to the tureen and serve them covered, to keep them hot. Serve with hot herb butter (p.47), and an assortment of breads.

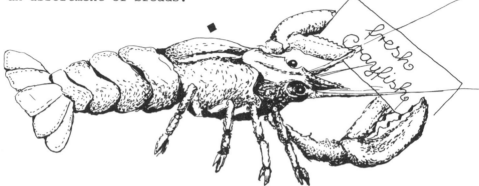

Poaching Liquid for Fish

In a poaching pan, mix 2 cups light wine vinegar, 2 cups white wine, and 4 cups water. Add the following ingredients: 3 onions cut in rings, 3 carrots, sliced, 1/2 celery root, cut into small bits, 1 large parsnip, slivered, 1 leek, cut in rings, some parsley stalks, without leaves, 1/2 lemon, untreated, sliced, 1 tsp juniper berries, 3 bay leaves, 1 tsp white peppercorns, 1/2 tsp mustard seeds, 3 whole cloves, 2 sage leaves, 1 tsp salt, 1/2 tsp sugar.

Simmer the broth 20 minutes before adding the fish. It is a matter of taste whether this broth is used for every kind of fish. In the restaurant "Schiffbäuerin" in Würzburg the broth is famous, as all kinds of fish are cooked together in the broth and lend it a special aroma. In the restaurant "Fischerrosl" in St. Heinrich on Lake Starnberg, a lighter or stronger tasting broth is prepared depending on the kind of fish, as directed by the chef.

Various Ways to prepare Fish

Poached Fish

Clean and draw the fish (tench, catfish, etc.), and wash it in a
bowl of water so as not to damage the skin. Douse the fish with
vinegar to obtain a blue coloring. Certain kinds of fish will
have to be scaled. Rub the inside of the fish with salt and
lemon juice. This will make the flesh firm. Place the prepared
fish in the warm broth and let it draw at low heat. When the
eyes of the fish protrude like white buttons and the fins can
be pulled out easily, the fish is done. Poaching time for
small fish is generally 8-10 minutes. Poached fish is
served on a platter, with boiled potatoes, and a bowl of melted
butter. The broth with the vegetables is served separately.

Sautéed Fish

Scale and draw the fish, wash it, dab it dry, sprinkle it well
with lemon juice, and let it draw. Then salt and lightly pepper
the fish, coat it with flour and put it in hot shortening (there
should be at least 1/3 in. shortening in the pan, less if the pan
is of the coated variety). Move the fish around a little immediately after putting it in the hot fat, so it does not stick to
the pan. Cooking time depends on the size of the fish: smaller
fish will take approx. 15 minutes, larger fish proportionately
longer, to cook. Serve garnished with lemon slices and parsley
sprigs and accompanied by a potato salad and other salads.

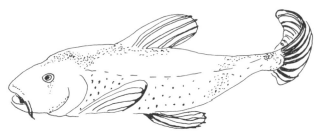

Fried Fish

Scale and draw the fish, wash it, dab it dry, sprinkle it well
with lemon juice, and let it draw. Then rub it with salt and pepper, dab it dry on the outside, coat it with flour, then with an
egg wash, and finally with stale bread crumbs mixed with semolina.

Regensburg Fish Sausages

In old times, the Regensburg Fish Kitchen was on White Cock Street "Weiße Hahnengasse" in Regensburg, right along the path leading to the historic Sausage Kitchen (Wurstküche) on the Danube. The fish sausages described here were a specialty. They taste just as good today.

1 1/2-2 lbs freshwater fish (whitefish)
2 1/2 oz. white bread
1 cup hot milk

Clean and bone the fish. Soak the bread in the milk, squeeze out the moisture and grind it in a meat grinder, along with the fish.

1 oz. butter
2 shallots, minced
3 Tbs parsley leaves, minced
1/2 lemon (untreated)

Cook the fish and bread mixture in the butter over moderate heat for a few minutes, adding the minced shallots, minced parsley leaves, and chopped (not grated!) lemon rind.

1/4 tsp marjoram

salt and pepper to taste
2 small eggs
1 Tbs thick cream

Season the cooked substance well and mix thoroughly with the eggs and cream. Form thumb-sized sausages.

2 eggs
stale breadcrumbs
shortening

Dip the sausages into the slightly beaten eggs, coat them with the breadcrumbs, and fry them to a crisp consistency in a frying pan.
Serve the fish sausages with potato salad, lettuce, and lemon wedges.

"Meefischle"

This dish is a typical Würzburg specialty, but it is surrounded by an aura of nostalgia nowadays, since such small fish can no longer be caught in large quantities.

In earlier times you were served a plate displaying a good dozen tiny fishes no larger than your ring finger. They were eaten whole, using your fingers; their heads and fins were particularly crisp.

Should you have the opportunity to get such tiny river fish, prepare them in the following manner:

2 lbs small
river fishes
salt
flour
coarse semolina
oil or shortening
lemon wedges

slit open the bellies of small fish, wash them well inside and outside, sprinkle with salt and coat them with a mixture of flour and semolina. Fry the fish in hot oil or shortening until crisp and nicely browned.

Drain well and serve them with lemon wedges, potato salad, and lettuce.

A generous glassful of wine from Franconia should accompany this delicacy.

Pike in Cream Sauce

1 large pike
lemon juice
1/4 lb smoked bacon,
cut in strips
salt & white pepper
parsley, lovage, dill,
tarragon, all chopped
6 thin slices smoked
bacon
1 onion, 1 carrot,
1 parsnip, 1 bay leaf,
2 slices lemon, un-
treated
1/2 cup dry white wine
1 cup thick sour cream

Count on approx. 3/4 lb fish per person. Clean and draw the pike, wash it thoroughly, and sprinkle it with lemon juice inside and outside. Using a larding pin, pull the bacon strips through the fish all the way along its back. Lightly salt the fish on the inside, and rub it with the pepper and the herbs. Line a large pan with the slices of bacon and place the fish on top of them. Add the vegetables, bay leaf and lemon slices to the pan. Cook in a preheated 450° F oven. When the bacon has melted, add the wine to the pan and pour the sour cream over the fish. Cooking time is 3/4 hours. Strain the sauce through a sieve, and serve the fish in the sauce, with boiled potatoes.

Ettal Trout

For 1 person:
1 brook trout
salt & pepper
1 sprig rosemary
1 sprig sage
frying fat or oil

Clean, draw, and wash the trout and rub it with salt and pepper inside and outside. Put the herbs in the belly of the fish. Brush the fish with melted frying fat or oil and put it in a well-oiled fish grill. Snap the grill closed, and stand it first at an angle to the glowing charcoal; then, when the heat has subsided, lay it flat and cook it on both sides until done. Serve the trout with fresh "Weissbier" (white beer), spicy "Bauernbrot" (peasant bread), and grated horseradish.

Vineyard Snails

Wherever wine grows there will also be vineyard snails, and they will have a delicious taste. So what if our German snails are first shipped to France, to be returned to us in cans?! Here is a recipe for gourmets:

As a first step, boil the snail shells in salted water, clean and dry them.

24 snails, canned

Arrange the snails in a deep bowl, adding just a little of the liquid from the can. Add the wine, and let the snails draw until you prepare the following dressing:

Herb butter:

3/4 lb butter

Stir the butter vigorously until foamy. Then add a mixture of the following herbs, finely chopped:

parsley, borage, lovage, thyme, tarragon, dill basil leaves, lemon verbena, and pimpernel

1/2 shallot
2 garlic cloves
salt
Cayenne pepper

Press or finely chop the shallot and the garlic cloves and add to the butter and herb mixture. Season with salt and Cayenne pepper, to taste.

Insert a snail into each shell. Using a teaspoon, fill the shells with the wine liquid and stop each shell with some of the herb butter. In a large snail pan, or in small individual snail pans, heat the snails on the top rack of a 460°F oven approx. 15 minutes or until the butter in the shells starts to bubble. Serve with toasted white bread, or tasty dark bread "Schwarzbrot". Set the the table with soup plates, soup spoons, snail tongs and snail forks. First pour the sauce from the shell into the spoon, then pull out the snail from the shell with the aid of the fork and eat it with the sauce.

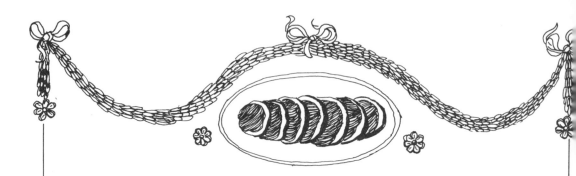

Meat Dishes

Roast Calf's Foot

1 calf's knuckle
1 garlic clove
salt & pepper

3 Tbs oil and
1 tsp butter
2 carrots
1/4 celery root
1 parsnip
1 lemon wedge
  (untreated)
rosemary
2 basil
  leaves
hot meat broth

Have the butcher split the calf's knuckle lengthwise. Wedge the garlic clove into the split bone. Remove some of the filament from the knuckle and rub it thoroughly with salt and freshly ground pepper. Place it into a covered roasting pan or heatproof dish. Preheat the oven to 470°F. Heat up the oil and butter and pour the mixture over the knuckle. Roast it briefly on each side, then turn the oven down to 420°F and continue to roast. Wash, clean, and coarsely cut up the vegetables, and add them to the roasting pan together with the lemon wedge, some rosemary to taste and the basil leaves. Cover with the lid or with aluminum foil. Baste once in a while with hot meat broth, scraping up the meat juices sticking to the pan, to mix with the broth. Roast for 1 1/2 hours (2 hours at most if the knuckle is very large). The gravy should be brown and clear and should not be bound with flour. Serve the calf's knuckle with bread dumplings (Semmelknödel) and lettuce.

Roast Veal

2 lbs veal (flat
shoulder)
salt & white pepper
4 Tbs oil &
2 Tbs butter
2 carrots
2 parsnip
1 lemon,untreated
hot broth
1 sprig lovage
1 sprig basil leaves

Wash and pat dry the meat, rub with salt
and pepper,and place it in a roasting pan.
Heat the oil and butter and pour over the
meat.Clean and coarsely cut up the vegetables,and arrange around the meat, together with a lemon wedge.Roast in a 450°F
oven for 1 1/2 hours,scraping up the juices sticking to the pan and basting con-
tinuosly with hot broth. Optional: add a
sprig each of lovage and basil leaves to
the gravy.Serve the gravy separately.Serve
roast veal with vegetables, potatoes and
salad; or mashed potatoes, "Spätzle", or
bread dumplings "Semmelknödel".

Roast Veal with Kidney

Serves 6 persons

Prepare 2 1/2 lb roasting veal which has been stuffed with
calf's kidney (ask for "Kalbsnierenbraten" at the butcher's),in
the same way as roast veal. It is advisable to take a large
roast,since it will be juicier than a small one.Cooking time:
1 1/2-2 hour.Serve with the same accompaniments as roast veal.

Stuffed Breast of Veal

Serves 7-8 persons

3 1/2 lbs breast
of veal
salt and pepper
3 white buns,finely
sliced
1/2 cup scalded milk
1 1/2 oz.butter
or oil
1 onion,chopped
2 Tbs parsley,chopped
1 lemon,untreated
1 egg and 2 yolks

Have the butcher cut a pocket into the
meat,and have him also remove any bones.
Wash and pat dry the meat and rub it inside and outside with salt and freshly
ground pepper.Soak the sliced buns in the
hot milk,covered,for 1/2 hour.In a saucepan heat the shortening,add the onion and
parsley and sauté the vegetables until
the onion is glassy.Add the finely chopped lemon rind,mix well,and fill the mixture loosely into the pocket of the meat.
Sew up the pocket,then roast the meat in
the same way as Roast Veal,above.Serve
with a mixed salad.

Veal in Sour Cream

2 lbs veal
(loin or shoulder)
salt and pepper
2 Tbs oil
6 slices bacon
2 carrots
1 parsnip
1 lemon wedge
(untreated)
1 tomato
hot meat broth
1 1/2 cups sour cream

Rub the meat with salt and pepper. In a roasting pan, fry the bacon in the oil until glassy, push the bacon slices to the side of the pan and brown the meat on all sides. Roast in a preheated 420°F oven, adding the coarsely cut up vegetables. Gradually add the meat broth and sour cream, scraping up the juices sticking to the pan. Cooking time is 1 1/2 hours. Remove the lemon wedge, puree the sauce through a sieve or in a blender. (No need to add flour as the sauce will be thick enough without it.) Serve with "Spätzle" or noodles.

"Catcall"

1 1/2 lb veal (leg,
shoulder, or breast)
salt and white pepper
2 oz. butter
2 Tbs flour
hot broth
1 egg yolk
2 Tbs cream
1 Tbs lemon juice
2 Tbs parsley, chopped
1 Tbs finely grated
lemon peel

Cut the meat into portions, sprinkle with salt and pepper, and brown very lightly in the butter. Sprinkle the meat in the pan with the flour, add the hot broth, cover, and braise the meat until tender. Turn off the heat, and mix in the egg yolk, cream, and lemon juice. Transfer the mixture to a bowl, sprinkle with parsley and grated lemon peel, and serve with noodles. A very light meal!

from
Anna
Fischer

Calf's Brains, Fried

Serves 2 persons

1 calf's brains
salt and pepper
flour (to coat)
1 egg
1 Tbs oil
1 Tbs cream
breadcrumbs
   (to coat)
frying fat or oil
lemon wedges

Wash the brains thoroughly in cold water.
Douse with hot water and carefully remove
the filaments. Season with salt and pepper
to taste, and coat with the flour. With a
fork, beat the egg with the oil and cream
in a shallow dish. Coat the brains first
with the egg mixture and then with the
breadcrumbs. Fry until crisp and golden
brown. Serve with fresh salads and lemon
wedges.

Munich Cutlets

4 pork cutlets,
   very lean
salt & pepper
horse radish, grated
   (fresh or prepared)
flour to coat
2 eggs, lightly
   beaten
stale bread crumbs
   to coat
oil to fry
parsley leaves,
   tomato & lemon
   slices

Lightly flatten the cutlets, season
them with salt and pepper, and coat
them thickly with the horse radish.
Dip them in flour to coat, and let
them dry briefly before quickly dipping
them in the eggs and subsequently
coating them with the breadcrumbs. In
a frying pan, heat enough oil to cover
the bottom well and fry the cutlets
at medium heat on both sides until
crisp. Garnish the cutlets with parsley
leaves, tomato and lemon slices, and
serve with a mixed salad.

Pork Ribs with Sauerkraut

1 1/2 lbs
Sauerkraut
4 pork ribs,
pickled & cooked

Prepare the Sauerkraut following the basic recipe on p.98.The prepared ribs may be bought at the butcher's.In a large saucepan,heat the Sauerkraut with the ribs and serve with mashed potatoes.This is a good dish for cooks pressed for time!

Black and White Pudding   Blut- und Leberwürste

White and black pudding is mostly eaten with Sauerkraut.Let the sausage draw in hot (but not boiling!) water for approx.20 minutes, and serve them on top of the Sauerkraut.

"Schlachtschüssel"

This is a dish combining several parts of the freshly killed pig, i.e.,sliced,boiled belly of pork,sliced,cooked,smoked pork,and white and black pudding,all served with Sauerkraut.Sometimes a grilled sausage "Bratwurst" is added to the meats.

Pork Tongue with Sauerkraut   Serves 2 persons

Prepare 1/2 portion vinegar broth as described in basic recipe, p.56.

2 pork tongues

Wash the tongues,place them in the boiling liquid to cover, and let simmer for 1-1 1/4 hour. Prepare the Sauerkraut as described in basic recipe (p.98), skin the tongues,slice them and arrange them on the Sauerkraut.Serve with boiled potatoes.

Pigs' Feet with Sauerkraut

"Knöchle" are pigs' feet chopped into bits.Since Sauerkraut takes less time to cook than the pigs' feet,it is recommended to cook the meat separately for approx.3/4 hour in salted water seasoned with 1 bay leaf and a few juniper berries,using this broth for cooking the Sauerkraut.Serve all mixed together in a deep dish.

Roast Pork I

2 lbs pork (shoulder
   or ham)
salt and pepper

2 medium onions,
   unpeeled
3 garlic cloves
2 Tbs caraway seeds

hot broth

cold, dark beer -or-
icewater

Wash and dry the meat and rub it with
salt and coarse, freshly ground pepper.
Using a sharp knife, cut a diamond
pattern into the rind. Fill a roasting
pan with approx. 1 in. water, and add
the meat, with the rind down. Cut the
onions into 1/5 in. rings, thinly slice
the garlic cloves and add to the meat.
Sprinkle with caraway seeds. Roast
the meat in a preheated 480° F oven
1/2 hour, then turn it around so that
the rind is on top and continue to
roast. Baste the meat frequently,
scraping up the juices sticking to the
pan and gradually adding some hot broth.
Total cooking time is approx. 1 1/2
hours. Toward the end of the cooking
time, brush the rind with cold, dark
beer or cold water, to make it crisp.
The gravy should be brown and clear
and should never be bound with flour
or starch: that would be a mortal sin
in Bavaria!

Roast Pork II

Prepare the meat in the same way
as Roast Pork I but without garlic,
add a pinch of majoram and a piece
of dark bread (Schwarzbrot) during
the roasting process.

Pig's Knuckle

Pig's knuckle is prepared like Roast Pork I. A large knuckle will
take 1 1/2-2 hours until done. During the first 1/2 hour of roasting, cover the roasting pan with aluminium foil. Set the oven at
450°F. Serve pig's knuckle with potato dumplings and Sauerkraut.

Vinegar Broth for Meat   Blausud

Vinegar broth should be well spiced, since it loses much of its strength in cooking. The amount of vinegar used depends on the acidity of the vinegar. For 8 cups watered-down light wine vinegar use the following ingredients:

3-4 yellow onions, sliced
3 carrots, sliced
1 parsnip, sliced
1/2 celery root, slivered
1/2 lemon, untreated, sliced
1 Tbs salt
1 tsp sugar
1/2 tsp black peppercorns
1/2 tsp juniper berries
4 bay leaves
4 whole cloves

Bring all ingredients to a strong boil before using the broth.

Calf's Tongue, sour   Serves 1-2 persons

Prepare 1/2 portion Blausud as described in basic recipe above.

1 calf's tongue

Wash the tongue, place it in the boiling liquid to cover, and let simmer for an hour or less (depending on the size and age of the tongue). Skin the tongue, beginning at the tip. Cut into medium-thick slices, decorate with the vegetable from the cooking liquid, pour some of the liquid over the meat and serve with plain boiled potatoes and horseradish or mustard.

vegetables from
"Blausud"
some cooking liquid

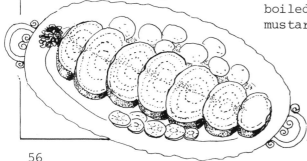

Veal Knuckle, Sour

Prepare a vinegar broth following the recipe on p. 56.

1 large veal knuckle	Have the butcher split the knuckle lengthwise. In a large, deep, heatproof dish, bring the vinegar broth to a boil, add the well-washed (and, if necessary, skinned) veal knuckle, and let simmer at low heat for 1 1/2-2 hours. Take out the knuckle, let it rest briefly, then carefully remove all meat from the bone, along the muscles. Replace the meat into the broth and reheat before serving. Serve with potatoes and mustard or horse-radish. This is a light meal.

Veal Stew, Sour

Serves 6 persons

Prepare a vinegar broth following the recipe on p. 56. Season to taste.

1 lb neck, round or shoulder of veal 1 sweetbread 1 veal tongue 1 calf's heart	Bring the broth to a boil. (It is best to use a large, deep heatproof dish which you can also use to serve the meal.) Add the meat, the sweetbread, tongue, and heart and let the meat simmer for 1 1/2-2 hours, taking the sweetbread from the broth earlier, then the tongue and heart, and then the meat. Skin the tongue, beginning from the tip. Cut the meat, sweetbread and heart in slices and serve together with broth vegetables and broth. This is best served with potatoes, or you might try serving it with dark bread.

Sweetbreads, Sour

Serves 1-2 persons

Prepare 1/2 portion "Blausud" as described in basic recipe p.56.

1 sweetbread Carrots and Onions from the"Blausud"	Wash the sweetbread, douse with boiling water, let stand for a minute, then drain and chill with cold water. Remove the filaments and skin, and let it simmer in the boiling "Blausud" to cover for 20 minutes. Serve with the carrots and onions from the "Blausud".

Meat Jelly

(Aspic)

This is a particularly refreshing dish in the summer."Genuine
Bavarian" meat jelly is not prepared with gelatine but is made
from calves' and pigs' knuckles. - Prepare a vinegar broth as
described in the basic recipe, p. 56.

Knuckle Jelly Knöcherlsulz

3 lbs calves'
and pigs'
knuckles,mixed
1 egg white

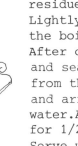

Have the butcher split the knuckles.Wash the
knuckles and put them in the cold broth in
a large pot. Bring to a boil and simmer for
approx.2 hours. Strain the liquid through a
sieve and let it settle for 1 hour,then pour
it into another pot carefully and discard the
residue.Bring the liquid to a boil again.
Lightly beat the egg white and mix it into
the boiling liquid.Take the pot from the heat.
After cooling, skim off the foam and scum
and season the liquid to taste.Remove meat
from the bones,cut it into small bits,
and arrange in a mold rinsed with cold
water.Add the liquid.Put in a very cold place
for 1/2 day,then unmold and cut into slices.
Serve with roast potatoes.

Roast Meat Jelly Bratensulz

1 lb lean roast
veal or pork
1-2 eggs,
hard -boiled
pickled gherkins

Cut the meat into 1/5 in.slices and arrange
the slices on a deep platter or plate,dec-
orating them with the sliced eggs, and
gherkins cut into "fans". Pour the jelly
liquid over the meat and put in a cold place
to set. Do not unmold.

Boiled Pork Tellersulz

Prepare a vinegar broth as described in basic recipe,p.56.

1 1/2 lbs lean pork   Add the pork to the boiling broth and
                      simmer for 3/4 hour.After cooling,cut the
meat into slices. Proceed as described in recipe for roast meat
jelly,above.

Calf's Lungs, Sour

Calf's lungs are not just a first course but,if you serve a salad first and a fruit dessert afterwards,they are a full meal. Prepare a strong "Blausud", p. 56.

1 calf's lung
1/2 calf's heart
5 oz.sweetbread
2 oz.shortening
1 Tbs sugar
4 Tbs flour
2 cups hot
"Blausud"
salt & pepper

Wash the lung,heart,and sweetbread well and add to the boiling "Blausud". Let it simmer for 3/4 hour (the sweetbread may be removed from the pot a short while before the other meat). Remove the filaments from the sweetbread. Place the lung between two plates to press and let it cool. After cooling, cut it into slices and then cut the slices into strips.Proceed in the same way with the heart (remove all fat) and the sweetbread. You may pour some of the liquid over the meat to cover and let it stand in a cool place overnight,or you may prepare a roux right away:

In a saucepan, heat up the shortening and the sugar and stir until brown. Add the flour and continue stirring until it is as brown as a hazelnut. Add some of the cold "Blausud", and stir until smooth,then pour in the hot liquid and stir to integrate. Add salt and pepper to taste. Let it simmer for 15 minutes (to get rid of the floury taste), then add the meat and heat up again. Serve with bread dumplings (Semmelknödel).

Braised Calf's Heart

1 calf's heart
salt & pepper

Wash the heart thoroughly,cut off some of the fat and rub with salt and pepper. Mix with:

1 carrot, 1 small parsley root, 1 small leek, rind of 1/2 lemon (untreated), parsley, lovage (all finely chopped).

3 Tbs oil
hot broth

Cut slits in the heart (see sketch). Fill the heart with the above mixture and fasten with skewers. Brown the heart in the oil on all sides, cover, and braise for 3/4 hour. Baste with hot broth if necessary.

Boiled Beef

This is a typical Bavarian dish, enjoying great popularity throughout the country.

2 lbs boiling beef (leg, brisket, rib, or shoulder)

Prepare Meat Soup, following basic recipe on p. 27 , but adding the meat after the water has come to a boil. Keep at a slow simmer to preserve the natural juiciness of the meat. Cooking time is 1 1/4-2 hours; in a pressure cooker the cooking time ist 35 minutes, but slow cooking is preferred, as it is easier to determine that way when the meat is done. When the meat is done, take it out of the soup and keep it warm, on a covered plate, to preserve the juices. Cut into slices just before serving, pour

chives, chopped

a little hot soup over the meat and sprinkle with chopped chives. Serve the boiled beef with potatoes (creamed or plain), spinach, Brussels sprouts, Savoy cabbage, grated horseradish, pickles, mustard or horseradish sauce. In Old Bavaria, boiled beef is also served with "Leberknödel" (liver dumplings) and a white radish salad. The hearty meat soup is served as a first course, garnished with thin noodles, small dumplings, chopped egg flan, etc.

Munich "Tellerfleisch"

Boiled Beef
chives, chopped
horseradish
2 dill pickles
1/2 tomato or
1 carrot, boiled
parsley sprigs

Prepare Boiled Beef as described in recipe, above. Place two or three slices of meat on a wooden plate and pour a little hot soup over the meat. Sprinkle with chives and horseradish and garnish with the sliced pickles. Add the tomato or carrot (taken from the soup and sliced) for color, and top with sprigs of curly parsley.

"Kronfleisch"

"Kronfleisch" or "crown meat" is a very delicate variety of Munich Boiled Beef "Tellerfleisch" made from the flank "flaches Kron" or "Zwerchfell" of the beef, which is cooked for just 10 minutes. It is even better if made from the short loin "dickes Kron" extending from the rib to the sirloin -- this is cooked for 3/4-1 hour in the same way as Boiled Beef, above.

Bœuf à la mode

2 lbs beef	Marinate the beef in a cold vinegar-and-red-wine marinade,p.78,for 3-4 days,then remove the meat, bring the liquid to a boil (reserving about 1 cup cold liquid),replace the meat and let it simmer
1 oz. butter	for approx. 1 hour or until tender. In a heavy
1 Tbs oil	saucepan, heat the butter with the oil,brown the
1 tsp sugar	sugar in the mixture,then add the flour and brown
4 Tbs flour	it. Add the reserved cold broth first,then some hot broth,altogether approx.3 cups. Let it simmer for at least 15 minutes. Cut the meat into slices, arrange the slices in a heatproof dish,

pass the sauce through a sieve, season to taste, and pour it over the meat. The sauce should be thick,smooth,and glossy.Serve with potato dollars,boiled potatoes,or bread dumplings (Semmelknödel).

Sour Beef

"Sauerbraten" is prepared in an entirely different way than Bœuf à la mode, although it is also marinated before cooking.

2 lbs beef (flat shoulder)	Marinate the beef in a cold vinegar-and-red-wine marinade,p.78, for 3-4 days,then
black pepper	remove the meat,wipe it dry,and rub it
1 Tbs oil	with freshly ground pepper. In a roasting
1/4 lb smoked, sliced bacon	pan in the oven preheated to 450°F,-cook the bacon until the fat has run out, then
1 large onion	add the meat,baste it with the fat, brown
1 carrot	it on all sides,and turn the oven down to
1/4 celery root	420°F. Add the coarsely cut up vegetables,
1 parsnip	sprinkle them with the flour,and let them
3 Tbs flour	brown alongside the meat. Baste with hot
hot marinade & broth	marinade and meat broth,as needed. Scrape
1 cup thick sour cream	up the pan juices and gradually add the sour cream. Cooking time is approx.1 1/2

hours. Remove the meat and keep it warm. Season the sauce to taste,pass it trough a sieve,and serve it separately. Arrange the meat on a heated platter.Serve with Spätzle,Klöß,potato dumplings, or noodles.

Leg of Lamb

Leg of lamb, called Lamperl, in the same way as kid (Geissle), is a traditional Easter dish in Bavaria. It tastes best if the meat is marinated for 1-2 days before cooking. Use the following marinade:

5 Tbs oil
2 garlic cloves
black pepper
1/4 tsp thyme
pinch of rosemary
2 1/2 lbs leg of lamb

1 onion
1 carrot
1/2 parsnip

hot broth

In a bowl, mix the oil with the pressed garlic cloves, freshly ground pepper, thyme and rosemary. Clean the leg of lamb carefully, removing all fat and, if you wish, removing the small lower bone. Wash the meat rapidly, wipe it dry, put it in the marinade, turn it a few times to coat, and refrigerate it for a day or two. -- Drain the meat in a colander. In a roasting pan, heat the marinade oil and brown the meat on all sides. Preheat the oven to 460°F. Add the coarsely cut up vegetables to the pan, cover, and roast 60 minutes in the oven, basting occasionally with hot broth. Let the meat rest for a while before carving. The meat should be pink on the inside. Serve with buttered string beans and parsley potatoes.

Saddle of Lamb

Saddle of lamb is prepared like leg of lamb. The cooking time is slightly less, approx. 40 minutes. Before removing the meat from the oven, remove the lid, turn the heat up to very high, baste the meat with the pan juices, and brown the saddle to a nice, rich color.

Kid

Serves 6 persons

Bavarians have three names for one small baby goat: Geissle, Kitzl, or Zicklein. Easter is the right time for serving this delicacy. If you have a whole kid, you may wish to stuff the rib part like a breast of veal, or cook it in a sour sauce, cut up into pieces, with the head, heart and milt (p. 57). The fore and hind legs are prepared like roast veal. Cooking time is 3/4-1 hour at the most, at 460°F. Serve kid with parsley potatoes, or bread dumplings (Semmelknödel), and fresh, green salads.

Fried Kid

A young animal may be prepared as is. An older one should be briefly blanched in boiling, spiced bone broth before coating, as it would become too dark on the outside during the frying process.

2 lbs kid legs
  (fore and hind)
salt and pepper
flour to coat
2 eggs, mixed with
1 Tbs oil or cream
stale bread crumbs
frying fat
lemon wedges

Cut the meat into portions, rub the pieces with salt and pepper, and coat them with flour. Dip the meat pieces in the egg wash, then coat thoroughly with the breadcrumbs, pressing them on. Heat a generous amount of shortening in a frying pan and fry the pieces of meat to a golden brown color. Drain them on paper towels and serve the fried kid decorated with lemon wedges and accompanied by potato salad, lettuce, and cucumber salad.

Tripe Squares

2 lbs tripe
salt
bone broth, p.32
1 calf's foot
2 garlic cloves
1 onion, studded with
3 whole cloves
5 peppercorns

white pepper, ground
salt
1 lemon (juice)
6 Tbs apple wine

Get the tripe from the butcher already cooked, or buy it raw and prepare it yourself, as follows: rub the tripe thoroughly with salt, let it soak in salted water, then rinse again, and simmer it slowly for at least 3 hours in a bone broth prepared with all ingredients listed alongside. (It takes much less time in a pressure cooker.) Cut the tripe into 2 in. squares, put them in a saucepan and keep them warm. Boil down the broth rapidly, uncovered, for approx. 20 minutes, season with white pepper, salt, lemon juice and apple wine, and pour it over the tripe squares. Serve with bread. You might also try to prepare tripe squares the Swabian way: follow the recipe for Sour Lung, p. 59 , make a dark roux, and add 1 Tbs raisins before serving.

Kidneys, Sautéed

You may use pork, beef or veal kidneys, as you prefer. The important thing is to soak the kidneys in milk at least an hour before cooking.

1 lb kidneys
1 large onion, finely chopped
1 1/2 oz. butter

salt and pepper
red wine to taste
  - or
Cognac to taste

After soaking the kidneys in milk, wash them quickly, halve them lengthwise. remove all filaments, and cut the kidneys in thin slices. Cook the chopped onion in the butter until it turns a light golden color, add the kidneys and sauté them rapidly at high heat, turning them to brown evenly (about 5 minutes). Just before serving add the salt and pepper and wine or Cognac. Serve with mashed or roast potatoes, and a salad.

Kidneys, Sour

Prepare the kidneys as in the recipe for sautéed kidneys but, after sautéeing them briefly, proceed as follows;

2 Tbs flour
approx. 1 cup hot broth
salt and pepper
1 Tbs vinegar

Sprinkle the flour on the kidneys in the pan, add the hot broth, salt, pepper and vinegar and heat up again stirring rapidly. You have to work quickly, otherwise the kidneys will become tough. Serve with roast or mashed potatoes.

Liver, Sautéed

1 lb calf's liver. Proceed as described in recipe for sautéed kidneys.

Liver, Sour

1 lb calf's liver. Proceed as described in recipe for sour kidneys.

Stuffed Pancakes

Prepare pancakes following the recipe on p. 142. Keep them warm. Prepare sauteed kidneys or liver as described above but without the sauce, stuff the hot pancakes with the meat and roll them up. Serve with salads for a light meal.

Ground Meat Dishes

Basic recipe:

1 stale bun
  soaked in milk
1 lb ground meat
  (beef, veal, and
  lean pork, mixed)
1 onion, finely
  chopped
1/2 lemon rind,
  grated (untreated)
2 Tbs parsley

Soak the bun in milk. In a small pan, warm the marjoram (heat enhances its flavor). In a large bowl, mix the meat with the bun (first squeeze out the milk as best you can), the onion, lemon rind, herbs and spices, and the eggs. Knead well, until it forms a smooth dough.

1/2 tsp salt	2 tsp marjoram
1/4 tsp pepper	2 eggs

Meat Patties   "Fleischpflanzl"

Shape the meat dough into balls weighing approx. 2 1/2 oz. and flatten the balls into patties. In a frying pan, fry the patties in oil or shortening on both sides until crisp (approx. 10 minutes). Serve with potatoes and a mixed salad, or with mashed potatoes and vegetables. Cold meat patties are also delicious and make a good outdoor snack or lunch to take to work.

Stuffed Cabbage

Prepare 1/2 portion meat dough following the basic recipe.

1 head white cabbage
  or Savoy cabbage
  (approx. 1-2 lbs)

Remove any damaged leaves from the cabbage. Put in a large pot filled with salted water, and bring to a brief boil (so the leaves can be easily separated).

Flatten the more prominent ribs with a knife. Spread the leaves. Mix the meat dough with 1 cup chopped cabbage, put 1 heaped Tbs on each leaf, fold in the long edges and roll up the leaves. Place the rolls in a well-buttered casserole dish, dot with butter flakes, and cook in the oven for 1/2 hour, at first covered, then uncovered.

1/2 cup sour cream
2 Tbs tomato paste

Beat the sour cream and tomato paste to mix and pour over the cooked cabbage rolls. Season to taste, and serve in the casserole, with mashed potatoes on the side.

Savoy
Cabbage

"Pichelsteiner"

The spelling is Pichelsteiner everywhere else, but Bavarians like things their own way ... Behind the name is a meat-and-vegetable stew which tastes best when you do not put everything in the pot at the same time, thus avoiding overcooking the vegetables. Proceed as follows:

1/2 lb beef (flat shoulder, or round)
1/2 lb pork (shoulder butt)
1/2 lb veal (shoulder)

Cut the meat into bite-size chunks. In a heavy saucepan, sauté 2 medium-sized onions, chopped, in 3 Tbs oil, until light golden and glassy. Add the meat, cover, and turn the heat low. Prepare the vegetables: peel and dice 4 medium potatoes, peel and cut into julienne strips 1 kohlrabi, 2 carrots and 1/2 celery root, slice 1 leek into rings. Wash and break into small bits 1 small head Savoy cabbage or 3/4 lb green beans. When you have prepared all vegetables, add them to the meat together with 1 tsp salt and 1/2 tsp pepper. Stir to mix. Bury 2 marrow bones in the mixture, add 1-2 cups meat broth, cover, and let the stew simmer in a preheated 380°F oven for a generous 1/2 hour. Just before serving, mix finely chopped herbs - parsley, basil leaves, lovage, and a small amount of savory - into the stew.

Rutabaga with Pork

2 lbs rutabagas
2 lbs pork bones
1/2 lb smoked pork

Wash and peel the rutabaga roots and slice them thinly, using a vegetable slicer. Put the sliced roots into a saucepan, arrange the meat on top of the vegetable and add water to barely cover the meat. Bring to a boil, turn down the heat, and simmer, covered, for 2 hours. No spices are needed for this dish, as the smoked meat supplies the taste. Serve with mashed potatoes.

from
Liesel Nöe

Accompaniments to Meat

Grated Horseradish

1/2 stick fresh horseradish

Grate the horseradish, holding the stick <u>tilted</u> to ensure that the gratings are <u>long</u>. Open the window, or you'll be in tears!

Delicate Horseradish Cream

1/4 stick fresh horseradish

1/2 orange
1/2 cup sweet cream

1 Tbs applesauce (optional)

Grate the horseradish, holding the stick straight to ensure that the gratings are <u>short</u>. Immediately sprinkle with the juice of 1/2 orange. Whip the cream until stiff and fold it into the horseradish. If you wish, you may add a little applesauce, mixing it in carefully.

Bamberg Horseradish

1/2 stick fresh horseradish
1 apple

1/2 lemon juice

Peel and grate the horseradish (short gratings). Peel and finely grate the apple, immediately dribble lemon juice over it and mix it with the horseradish.

Horseradish Sauce, warm

1 oz. butter
1 Tbs oil
3 Tbs flour
1/2 cup cold milk

1 1/2 cups hot broth

1/2 stick horseradish

In a saucepan, heat the butter and oil, stir in the flour, toast to a light golden color, stirring all the time. Remove from heat, add the milk and stir vigorously to avoid clotting. Add the broth, stirring, bring to a boil, and simmer for 10-15 minutes. Grate the horseradish (short gratings) and add to the liquid. Reheat and serve immediately.

Mustard Sauce

3 eggs

3 medium sweet-sour
   pickled gherkins
salt and pepper to taste
3 Tbs sweet mustard
warm broth
1-2 Tbs grated (short)
   horseradish
chives
parsley   chopped
dill

Cook the eggs 10 minutes, chill
them in cold water, peel them and
chop them small (you may use an
egg slicer for this, placing the
eggs into it crosswise first and
then lengthwise). Put the chopped
eggs in a bowl. Add horseradish.
Chop up the gherkins finely and
add to the eggs together with the
salt, pepper, and mustard. Mix
with a small quantity of broth and
season with plenty of chives,
parsley and dill.

Cranberry Preserve

Tastes particulary good with game or
"Sauerbraten".

10 lbs cranberries
3 lbs sugar
1/2 cup water
1 lb ripe pears

pure alcohol

Pick over the berries and wash them.
Drain, Use a large, wide saucepan
to cook berries together with the
sugar and water. Peel, core, and
cut the pears in pieces, and add
them to the berries. Let simmer
for 20 minutes. Fill in screw-top
jars rinsed with alcohol. If you
have no cool storage place, the
cranberry preserve may also be
sterilized. It can also be used
in desserts (p.130).

Suckling Pig

It should be noted that an individually roasted piece of meat, whether leg or shoulder, will never taste as good as a whole suckling pig baked at the baker's or roasted on an open-air spit.

1 suckling pig
salt and pepper
1 tsp caraway seed, ground

dark beer
melted butter

Rub the outside of the pig with salt only, the inside with salt, pepper, and crushed caraway seed. Let draw at least 2 hours. Wrap the ears, tail and feet in aluminum foil. Roast the pig on a spit 2-3 hours, turning it as necessary and basting frequently with dark beer and melted butter, until crisp. Pierce with a fork once in a while to avoid blistering of the skin. Remove the aluminum foil before serving. Serve with sweet mustard, cabbage salad, potato salad, and a large selection of breads.

from Irma Rössner Munich

Ham in Bread Dough

8 lbs raw ham
3 lbs rye bread dough from the baker's

8-10 Pers.

A nicely marbled ham will be juicier; choose one that is not too salty or too strongly smoked. Keep the dough cool and do not let it rise. Roll it out to a thickness of just under 1 in., and wrap the ham into it completely, like a package. Place on a larded and floured baking sheet. Using a thick pin, pierce holes into the dough to allow the steam to escape. Bake at 490°F for 2 1/2 hours, until crisp.

Roast Goose

Roast Goose is served at Church Fair time, on the feast of St. Martin, and at Christmas. It is hard to break with this tradition in Bavaria. Not even the turkey has succeeded in doing so!

1 goose
salt & pepper,
mixed

Soak the goose 1/2 day in cold water, drain and pat dry. Should it still have some down and quill ends: pour a small mound of salt onto a small plate, wet it with methylated spirit, light it, and singe all remaining down and quill ends. Cut off the neck and wings and put them aside, along with the gizzard, the liver, and all removable fatty clots, for other use. Rub the goose very thoroughly, inside and outside, with a mixture of salt and pepper, cover it with a cloth, and place it in the cold oven for a night's sleep.-- When you are ready to cook the goose, pour a good inch of boiling water into the roasting pan of the oven, preheat the oven to 400°F, and place the goose, with its back up, on the oven grill. When the back has browned, the goose is turned around. Prick the goose lightly under the legs to allow the fat to escape. This should then be skimmed and reserved in a small pot or glass. Baste the goose frequently throughout the roasting process, scraping up the juices sticking to the pan. If you need to add water to the juices, always add it hot and never pour it over the goose! Cooking time is 2 1/2-3 hours, depending on the size of the goose. It should be possible to move the legs about lightly, when the goose is done. Toward the end of the roasting time, turn the heat up to 470°F, and brush the goose with ice-cold salted water, to make the skin very crisp. Let the goose rest a while before carving, then halve it and carve in the usual way. The plates should always be preheated when serving roast goose. Serve the goose the Old Bavarian way with raw potato dumplings, celery root and lamb's lettuce, or the Franconian way with red cabbage, "Klöss", and apple sauce.

Roast Chicken

You will find the chicken under many names in Bavaria: Gockerl, Brathendl, Hähnchen, Mistkratzer, Gickel and Göcker, depending on the region you are visiting. In all parts of Bavaria it is mainly served in its roast variety, although lately, it has also become the fashion to grill it. The most important thing about a chicken is where it comes from: a free-running chicken will have firm and plump meat and a crisp skin when roasted. The late lamented Aunt Augusta made the best roast chicken this way:

2 chickens,
1 1/2-2 lbs ea.
salt & pepper
2 bunches parsley
2 tsp butter
boiling broth
2 carrots
1 parsnip
1 sprig lovage
melted butter
cold salted water

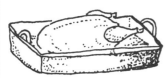

Wash, drain, and pat dry the chickens, and rub them on the inside with salt and freshly ground pepper. Wash and drain the parsley, and stuff a bunch into the tummy of each chicken, along with the gizzards, the hearts, and 1 tsp butter. Preheat the oven to 470°F. Place the chickens on the oven grill, fill the roasting pan of the oven with boiling broth, adding the greens.
Baste the chickens frequently throughout the roasting process (approx. 1 hour). Toward the end of the roasting time, brush the chickens with ice-cold salted water to make the skin crisp. In Old Bavaria, roast chicken is served with bread dumplings ("Semmelknödel") and various salads.

Roast Duck

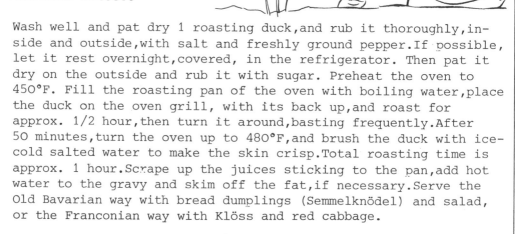

Wash well and pat dry 1 roasting duck, and rub it thoroughly, inside and outside, with salt and freshly ground pepper. If possible, let it rest overnight, covered, in the refrigerator. Then pat it dry on the outside and rub it with sugar. Preheat the oven to 450°F. Fill the roasting pan of the oven with boiling water, place the duck on the oven grill, with its back up, and roast for approx. 1/2 hour, then turn it around, basting frequently. After 50 minutes, turn the oven up to 480°F, and brush the duck with ice-cold salted water to make the skin crisp. Total roasting time is approx. 1 hour. Scrape up the juices sticking to the pan, add hot water to the gravy and skim off the fat, if necessary. Serve the Old Bavarian way with bread dumplings (Semmelknödel) and salad, or the Franconian way with Klöss and red cabbage.

Stuffed Pigeons

4 pigeons
salt & pepper
3 white buns
(2-3 days old)
1/2 cup hot milk
2 Tsp. butter
1 small onion,chopped
1 bunch parsley,
chopped
1/2 lemon rind,untreated
2 lorage leaves,
pigeon livers & hearts,
1 egg & 1 egg yolk
1 Tbs oil
2 Tbs butter
1 carrot, cut into
coarse pieces
1 parsnip,cut into
coarse pieces
1 1/2 cups hot broth

Wash the pigeons quickly,pat dry and rub inside and outside with salt and pepper. Cut the buns into thin slices, pour the hot milk over them and let soak,covered,for 1/2 hour.In a sauce-pan,heat up the butter,add the greens, herbs,and the chopped livers and sauté the mixture briefly.

Add egg and egg yolk to soaked buns, mix,add the sautéed mixture,mix every-thing well,and fill the pigeons with this stuffing. Close the cavities with skewers,or sew them up. In a flat saucepan,heat the oil and butter, add the pigeons, and brown them lightly on each side. Add carrot and parsnip pieces,cover,and cook the pigeons on top of the stove,or in a preheated 420 F oven,for approx. 1 hour. Grad-ually add some hot broth,as necessary. Strain the gravy through a sieve, pressing down on the vegetables with a spoon to extract all juices,and serve the gravy separately. Let the pigeons rest before serving,keeping them warm. Then cut them in half lengthwise and serve them with finely seasoned salads and vegetables. A nice way to serve them is to prepare a double portion of the bun dough,form the leftover half into small (approx.1 1/2 in.dia.) dumplings,simmer them 15 minutes in salted water, drain and serve with the pigeons.

Game

To prepare game:
Whether game is to be marinated or not, is a matter of taste. The meat of older animals should, however, be marinated in a vinegar & red wine marinade. Deep-frozen game should not be marinated. To season deep-frozen meat, prepare it before freezing, as follows: dip a linen or cotton cloth into red wine vinegar and sprinkle it with the various game spices. Clean the meat thoroughly, removing all membranes, roll it up tightly in the cloth, put it in a freezer bag, seal the bag tightly and freeze it. It is better if you do not lard the game: larding causes too much meat juice to escape from the meat, whereas the application of hot slices of bacon, as described in the recipes, will have the effect of sealing the pores of the meat, making it tender and juicy. The sauce is generally made thick and smooth by the addition of thick cream; therefore, cream is to be added in portions right after the meat has been browned on all sides. If you need a lot of sauce for several people, don't just add flour to the sauce! Rather, brown 1 tsp sugar in a mixture of 3 Tbs cooking oil and 1 Tbs butter, and brown 3 Tbs flour in this mixture. Add some of the marinade, stir to dissolve any lumps, add some thick cream and red wine, and simmer for 15 minutes. The result is worth the effort! Another thing to keep in mind: saddle and leg have different cooking times - do not cook them together in the same pot! If no marinade is used, add the marinating spices to the sauce to taste. The addition of fresh or dried mushroom to the sauce will also enhance its taste.

Saddle of Venison

The meat should either be marinated, using a red wine vinegar marinade (p. 78), or it should be rolled into a cloth dipped in vinegar, or soaked in buttermilk, for 4 days.

1 saddle of venison
pepper, salt
juniper berries
8 slices smoked
bacon
2 Tbs oil
onions, carrots,
celery root, parsnip
1 bay leaf
1-1 1/2 cups
thick sour cream
marinade or broth
red wine

Clean the meat, removing all membranes. Rub the meat with pepper, very little salt, and some crushed juniper berries. Preheat the oven to 450°F. In a roasting pan on top of the stove, lightly fry the bacon in the oil. Cover the saddle with the bacon slices and brown carefully on all sides to seal in the juices. Add the coarsely chopped vegetables and bay leaf. Roast the meat, still covered with the bacon slices, but without a lid, in the oven for 1-1 1/2 hours or until tender (roasting time depends on the age of the animal). Scrape up the meat juices sticking to the pan throughout the roasting process, gradually adding some sour cream, and a little marinade or broth. A small amount of red wine can do no harm! In Franconia, some bread rind is added to the sauce to thicken it.

When the meat is done, let it rest, covered, for 5 minutes, then carve it with a very sharp knife. Assemble the meat once again along the ribs, decorate with mushroom heads and surround it with stewed pear halves filled with cranberry preserve. Serve with red cabbage and potato dumplings, or in Lower Bavarian fashion, with bread dumplings, Semmelknödel, or in Franconian way, with Klöss, or as they do in Swabia, with Spätzle.

Leg of Venison

has tougher meat than the saddle and should be marinated. Then cook like the saddle, above, for approx. 90 mins. If you wish to serve a

Cold Saddle of Venison

prepare the meat as described above but do not add any sour cream. Boil down the clear sauce rapidly and baste the meat often with it, to make it a nice, glossy brown.

Leg of Wild Boar

1 leg of a young
wild boar
salt & pepper
juniper berries,
crushed
oil
3 onions
2 carrots
1 pc. celery root
hot broth
bread rind or
2 Tbs flour
1 liqueur glass gin
1 cup sour cream

Soak the well-hung leg of a young wild boar in buttermilk for 5 days, then rub thoroughly with salt, pepper, and crushed juniper berries. In a heavy roasting pan, heat up enough oil to cover the bottom well, and brown the meat on all sides. Add the coarsely cut-up vegetables and roast in a preheated 420°F oven, uncovered, for approx. 2 hours, basting frequently. Add some hot broth, scrape off the juices sticking to the pan, and mix in some bread rind or 2 Tbs flour, to taste. Purée the sauce. As a final touch, add the gin and sour cream. Serve with red cabbage, potato dollars, any kind of dumplings, mashed potatoes, or "Spätzle".

Saddle of Wild Boar

1 saddle of a young
wild boar
salt, pepper,
thyme
5 Tbs oil
2 onions
1 cup sour cream
1 cup red wine

Remove the fat from the meat and marinate the meat 4-5 days in a strong red-wine marinade (p. 78). Then wipe the meat, rub it thoroughly with salt, pepper, and thyme, and brown on all sides in a roasting pan, together with the coarsely cut-up onions. In a preheated 420° F oven, roast the meat for 1-1 1/2 hours. Baste occasionally, gradually adding the heated-up marinade, the sour cream and red wine, and scraping off the juices sticking to the pan. A piece of dark bread rind may be cooked along in the pan, to thicken the sauce. Purée the sauce, and serve with red cabbage, baked apples filled with cranberry preserve, chanterelles or other mushrooms, and dumplings.

from
Hil de Bieber
Würzburg

Saddle of Hare

Serves 2 persons

1 saddle of hare
salt, pepper
juniper berries
1/4 lb smoked
streaky bacon
slices
2 Tbs oil
1 carrot, peeled
and coarsely cut up
1 small onion,
coarsely diced
hot marinade
1 cup thick
sour cream
red wine

Clean the meat, removing all membranes. Roll it in a cloth dipped in vinegar, or soak it in buttermilk, for a few days, or marinate it (below). Then wipe it dry and rub it with pepper, very little salt, and some crushed juniper berries. Cut in slightly between the vertebrae, or stick skewers through them, to keep the saddle straight. In a wide pan, lightly fry the bacon slices in the oil, push them to the side of the pan, add the saddle top side down and brown it lightly. Turn the saddle around, arrange the bacon slices on it to cover, and add the carrot and onion to the pan. Roast in a preheated 430° F oven for 20 minutes, covered, then take off the lid and continue to roast, gradually adding portions of marinade and sour cream, and scraping up the juices sticking to the pan, for a total roasting time of approx. 1/2 hour. Add red wine to taste. Pass the sauce through a sieve and serve it separately. Carve the meat, cutting along the spine and carefully loosening the meat from the ribs. Slice the meat and reassemble it on the ribs. Serve with cranberry preserve, stuffed, stewed pears, "Spätzle" or dumplings and red cabbage.

Vinegar – Red Wine Marinade

1 1/2 cups red wine vinegar
1 1/2 cups red wine
1 1/2 cups water
1 tsp salt

8 peppercorns
3 bay leaves
4 whole cloves
8 juniper berries

2 onions, sliced
2 carrots, cleaned and sliced
1 celery root, slivered

Bring all ingredients to a boil and let them simmer 10 minutes. Let the mixture cool and pour over the game or other meat to cover.

Leg of Hare

4 legs of hare
juniper berries
salt and pepper
2 Tbs oil
7 oz. smoked
streaky bacon,
sliced
1 onion, diced
1 carrot,
coarsely cut up
hot marinade
1-1 1/2 cups thick
sour cream

Clean the legs, removing all membranes,and marinate 2 days in marinade or buttermilk. Dry the legs thoroughly and rub them with the crushed juniper berries, very little salt, and pepper. In a heavy, wide saucepan, heat up the oil and lightly fry the bacon slices. Push the bacon to the side of the pan and add the legs, browning them lightly on each side. Add the onion and carrot. Let the legs simmer, covered, on top of the stove or in the oven. (Game will dry out quickly if allowed to cook uncovered.) Baste with hot marinade, if necessary, and gradually add the sour cream. Cooking time is approx. 1 hour at 430°F.

Leg of hare is typically served with Spätzle, cranberry preserve, red cabbage. In Lower Bavaria it is served with bread dumplings,Semmelknödel, and in Franconia with Klöss.

Wild Duck

Prepare the stuffing by mixing well the following ingredients:

2 apples,peeled and cut into thick slices
1 Tbs raisins

1 Tbs walnut meat, coarsely chopped
3 Tbs stale dark breadcrumbs
3 Tbs brandy

1 wild duck, cleaned
salt, pepper, thyme
2 oz. butter or oil,
heated
hot broth
red wine and cream

Rub the inside and outside of the duck with salt, pepper, and thyme, stuff it with the above mixture, and sew it up. Preheat the oven to 470°F. In a casserole, pour the hot shortening over the duck and let the duck roast in the oven approx. 1 hour, basting it occasionally with hot broth and scraping up the juices sticking to the pan.After roasting,add red wine and cream to taste. Serve with mashed potatoes or potato dollars,red cabbage, and cranberry preserve.

Pheasant

1 pheasant
brandy
2 oz. mushrooms,
dried
salt & pepper
6 pcs. zwieback
1 cup milk
1 onion, chopped
1 oz. butter
2 Tbs parsley,
finely chopped

Rub the pheasant with brandy inside and outside and refrigerate 2 days.
Soak the mushrooms in lukewarm water. Rub the pheasant with salt and pepper inside and outside. Soak the zwieback in milk, squeeze and put in a bowl. Lightly sauté the onion in the butter, add the chopped liver, heart and gizzard of the pheasant as well as the squeezed and coarsely chopped mushrooms and the parsley, and sauté the mixture briefly. Add the mixture to the zwieback and season to taste. Stuff the pheasant and close the aperture with skewers or thread.

4-6 slices
smoked bacon

Wrap the bird in bacon slices, and truss it up with thread.

hot broth
1 bay leaf,
crumbled
1 onion, chopped
1 carrot, chopped

In a roasting pan, roast the pheasant in a preheated 450° F oven approx. 1 hour, basting frequently. Place the crumbled bay leaf and coarsely chopped onion and carrot alongside the meat in the pan, and add hot broth as necessary.

Serve with wine sauerkraut (p. 98) and mashed potatoes (p. 103).

Recipe from
Straubing

Partridge

4 young partridges	Wash the partridges on the outside,wipe them lightly inside with a moist,clean rag.Rub
salt & pepper	them inside and outside with a little salt,
juniper berries, crushed	pepper,thyme and crushed juniper berries.Remove the cores of the unpeeled apples and
thyme	place an apple inside each bird.Wrap the
4 small apples	partridges in the bacon slices and truss them up with thread.In a roasting pan,heat
appr. 1/2 lb smoked streaky bacon,sliced	the oil and lightly brown the birds on all sides until the bacon is glassy.Cover and roast in a preheated 470°F oven 40 minutes.
1 Tbs oil	Gradually add the cream and,if necessary, some hot broth,scraping up the juices stick-
1 cup heavy cream	ing to the pan.Strain the sauce through a sieve.Serve with wine sauerkraut (p.98) and
hot broth	mashed potatoes (p.103).

Partridges

that are past their prime may be recognized by their grey feet. Cook them in the following manner:

Prepare 1/2 recipe red wine marinade (p.78).

4 old partridges	Clean and season the birds as described above.Bring the marinade to a boil,add the
1/2 lb streaky bacon, sliced	partridges and simmer gently 1/4 hour.Then wrap them in bacon slices, truss them up with thread,and roast them as described above.
	Roasting time: approx. 1 hour.

from
Aunt Gusti.

Roast Snipe

Snipes should always be plucked from the head down, to avoid damaging the skin. After plucking the birds, draw them, wash the bowels very well and soak them in water. Wash the gizzards, hearts, etc. and put them aside.

4 snipes
salt & pepper
pinch of marjoram
4 Tbs red wine
1 Tbs sugar
1 Tbs lemon juice
approx. 1/2 lb
bacon, raw, un-
smoked, sliced

1 onion, coarsely
chopped
hot broth

Rub the snipes, inside and outside, with salt, pepper, and marjoram. Mix the red wine with the sugar and lemon juice and rub the insides of the snipes with the mixture. Cover the outside of each snipe with bacon slices and truss them with thread to keep the bacon in place. Preheat the oven to 450°F. In the meantime, in a saucepan on top of the stove, cook the snipes on each side until the bacon becomes glassy. Add the onion to the pan, cover, and roast in the oven for 1/2 hour. Baste with a red wine-lemon juice mixture (see above) and some hot broth, as necessary. Before serving, remove the bacon slices, and strain the gravy through a sieve.

Sautéed Snipe's Gizzards

And here is the hors d'oeuvre to serve before roast snipe: Sautéed Snipe's Gizzards ("Schnepfendreck")

Dry the thoroughly washed and soaked bowels of the snipes (see above), and chop them up very finely, together with the livers, gizzards, and hearts.

1 oz. butter
1 shallot, finely
chopped
2 Tbs parsley,
chopped
salt
nutmeg
white bread rounds

Lightly sauté the shallot in the butter, add the parsley and chopped meat, and sauté the mixture briefly. Season with salt and nutmeg, to taste. Toast the bread rounds, spread them with butter, and top each round with the sautéed meat mixture. Serve hot.

Endive Salad (Cichorium endivia)

There are many kinds of endive, but they are all prepared in the same manner. Endive salad is particularly favored as a winter green.

2 large endives	Remove the stalks and outer leaves of the endives. Wash the endives rapidly but thoroughly in luke-warm salted water and cut them into narrow strips.
1 clove garlic 3 Tbs salad oil	Rub the inside of a salad bowl with the garlic, put the endive strips into the bowl and mix with the oil.
1 Tbs herb mustard 3 Tbs red wine vinegar 2 Tbs cream 1 Tbs red onion, chopped 1 Tbs parsley, chopped	In a bowl, beat the liquids to blend, pour them over the endives, add the onion and parsley and mix. Correct the taste, as needed.

Endive Salad Franconian recipe

Prepare the endives as described above, and add the following dressing:
2-3 Tbs vinegar
salt to taste
pepper to taste
1 onion, chopped
2-3 Tbs salad oil
1 potato,boiled,peeled & grated

Mix all ingredients thoroughly and add to endives.Mix carefully and correct taste, as needed.

Lettuce (Latuca sativa)

In Bavaria, lettuce is called simply "green salad," and may be found on every salad plate in restaurants. In private households it is prepared in larger quantities and with more loving care. Use only fresh salad -- it quickly loses its value when exposed to light and heat.

1-2 heads lettuce — Clean the lettuce and cut off the stalk. Wash rapidly in salted water and shake dry in a colander. The larger leaves may be separated along the center "rib."

2 Tbs wine vinegar
3 Tbs oil
pinch of salt
3 Tbs herbs: parsley, lovage, borage, dill, lemon verbena, chives (all chopped)

Beat together the vinegar, oil and salt, pour over the lettuce, add the herbs, and mix. You may also add:

1 small onion, chopped (Optional) or small red radishes, sliced (Optional) or garden cress (Optional)

Serve immediately after adding the dressing!

Watercress Salad (Nasturtium officinalis)

Watercress grows abundantly in the small creeks of Bavaria. It is best when freshly picked. It may be mixed with lettuce, or prepared by itself. The coarse stalks should be removed as they taste somewhat bitter. This is a healthy salad for people with weak stomachs!

3/4 lb watercress — Wash the watercress in salted water. Drain well.

3 Tbs red wine vinegar
3 Tbs olive oil
salt to taste
1/2 tsp mustard

Beat together the vinegar, oil, salt and mustard, pour over watercress and mix. You may also add:

1 small red onion, chopped
1 hard-boiled egg, chopped . (Optional)

Green Bean Salad

This may be made from any kind of string beans, although preparation time varies slightly with the type of beans used. To keep their fresh, green color, the beans should be chilled ("shocked") with ice-cold water right after cooking.

1 lb beans	Clean and wash the beans and boil them in lightly salted water for 10-12 minutes or until just tender. Do not overcook! Drain in a colander and chill with ice-cold water. Drain well, place in salad bowl, and season with following sauce:

2 Tbs red wine vinegar
1/4 tsp dry mustard
1 Tbs red wine
1/4 tsp ground black pepper
3 Tsp salad oil

In a cup, mix well all ingredients and pour over beans. Mix gently but thoroughly. Let the salad draw for approx. 1 hour. Just before serving, sprinkle the salad with

1 small onion, finely chopped
1 tsp parsley, finely chopped
1 tsp savory, finely chopped

Lamb's Lettuce (Valerianella locusta L.)

1/2 lb lamb's lettuce

Clean the lettuce carefully, removing the small roots. Wash thoroughly in lightly salted water and, in a colander, shake well to remove all water. Place loosely in a bowl and season with following sauce:

2 Tbs vinegar
3 Tbs salad oil
1/2 clove garlic, pressed
1/2 tsp mustard
1/4 tsp salt
1 small onion, finely chopped
5 red radishes, finely sliced

In a cup, mix well all ingredients and pour over lettuce. Mix gently but thoroughly.

(Optional)

White Radish Salad (Raphanus sativua)

Bavarians prefer to use radishes grown in the village of Weichs near Regensburg, where they grow particularly tender. Sometimes the Danube "helps" the gardeners by overflowing its banks and watering the radish beds thoroughly.

1 large radish
  - or -
2 small radishes
1 Tbs light vinegar
2 Tbs oil
salt to taste
black pepper

Scrape the radishes and slice thinly on a vegetable slicer, or grate them. Mix with the vinegar, oil, and salt. Sprinkle with freshly ground pepper.

Red Radish Salad

4-5 bunches small
  red radishes
5 Tbs sweet cream
1 Tbs herb vinegar
salt to taste
chives, chopped

Cut off the leaves of the radishes, wash them well, and grate or slice them on a vegetable slicer. Add the cream, vinegar and salt, mix well, sprinkle with chives and serve immediately.

Cucumber Salad

Lower Bavarian recipe

1 large cucumber
1 white radish
1 Tbs light vinegar
salt   )
pepper) to taste
2 Tbs olive oil
chives, chopped

Carefully peel the cucumber, scrape off the crust of the radish, and slice both on a vegetable slicer. Mix well with the vinegar, salt, and freshly ground pepper, sprinkle with the chives, and serve immediately, as this salad is hard to digest if left standing too long.

Cucumber Salad (Franconian recipe)

1 large cucumber
4 Tbs sour cream
1 Tbs light vinegar
salt   )
pepper) to taste
3 borage leaves, cut
   into strips
1 tsp dill, chopped

Carefully peel the cucumber and slice on a vegetable slicer. Pour the sour cream and vinegar over the cucumber and season with salt and freshly ground pepper. Add the borage and dill, mix well, and serve immediately.

Potato Salad with Cucumber

Prepare the potato salad as described below.

1 cucumber
1 Tbs dill, chopped

Peel the cucumber and cut it into not-too-thin slices, using a cucumber slicer. Mix into the prepared potato salad. Sprinkle with the dill.

Potato Salad

2 lbs potatoes

Use boiling potatoes (the kind of potato that retains its shape when cooked) for this recipe. Boil the potatoes in their jackets (see p. 100) and peel while still hot. Slice the potatoes thinly and mix with the finely

1 large onion
2 cups meat stock,
   hot
6 Tbs light
   vinegar
1 tsp salt
3-4 Tbs oil
black pepper to
   taste
chives, chopped

chopped onion. In a small bowl, blend the vinegar and salt, pour the mix over the potatoes and mix loosely. Put in a warm place to draw for at least 1 hour. Just before serving, add the oil to the salad and mix gently but thoroughly. Decorate with freshly ground pepper and chives. Potato salad should always be served lukewarm.

Celery Root Salad, cooked

3 large celery roots

Brush the celery roots well under running water. Cut off the greens and fibrils. Put in cold water in a potato steamer or pressure cooker, bring to a boil, and cook until cooked through but still firm. Do not over-cook! Peel while still hot, slice, and place into a shallow dish. Douse immediately with the salad sauce. The celery slices should be completely covered by the sauce to avoid discoloration.

2 cups hot water
1/2 cup light vinegar
1/4 tsp celery salt

Mix all ingredients well und pour over the sliced celery. Let draw at least a few hours, preferably over-night.

3 Tbs oil
black pepper to taste
chives, chopped

Just before serving, add the oil and freshly ground pepper, mix, and sprinkle with chives. This is the traditional salad to serve with roast goose, since it not only tastes well, but also makes the rich goose-meat more digestible.

Celery Root Salad, raw

6 Tbs plain yoghurt or
  "gestöckelte" milk
1 Tbs sweet cream
2 Tbs oil
celery salt, to taste
6 oz. celery root, raw
1 large, juicy apple
2 oz. walnut meat,
  coarsely chopped

In a salad bowl, beat together the yoghurt (or "ge-stöckelte" milk), cream, oil and celery salt. Clean, peel and grate the raw celery, clean, peel and grate the apple, and add both to the sauce. Add the chopped walnuts. Mix well. This salad tastes good with cold meat.

White Cabbage Salad (Brassica ol. var. capitata)

This tastes best when made with fresh,young,white cabbage,which still has a greenish hue.Although some like it scalded,gourmets prefer it unscalded,preserving its distinctive taste and high vitamin content.

1 head white
cabbage
about 1-1/2 lbs
4-5 tsp
vegetable oil

Quarter the cabbage head,removing stalk.Wash thoroughly in salted water.Drain well.By hand,or using a vegetable slicer,cut into fine strips. Place in bowl and mix well with the oil,until the strips become shiny. Cover and let stand for 1 hour.

1/2 cup light-colored
vinegar
1 1/2 cups warm water
1 tsp salt
1/4 tsp black pepper
coarsely ground
1 tsp caraway seeds,
coarsely ground

In a cup,mix well all ingredients and pour over cabbage. Cover, and let draw for 1-2 hours.

2 oz. lean bacon (optional)

Just before serving,garnish the seasoned salad with diced bacon, fried,and drained on paper towels.

Red Cabbage Salad

In Bavaria, red cabbage is called blue cabbage -- This salad is prepared in the same way as white cabbage salad (see above).The seasoning may be enhanced by adding to the sauce a pinch of ground cloves, and mixing into the salad

1 small apple, cut into slivers
1 small red onion, chopped

Asparagus Salad

Arrange the cooked asparagus in an oblong glass dish or on a deep plate. Prepare a marinade; this may have a strong taste, since asparagus will absorb much of it. The spices should be well balanced, however, to preserve the delicate taste of the vegetable. If you wish, you may halve the asparagus spears crosswise before cooking; they will fit better on salad plates that way.

For the marinade, use the water in which you boiled the asparagus. For every 2 cups of asparagus water (use while still hot!) take:

approx. 4 Tbs light vinegar
2 Tbs dry white wine
1 pinch white pepper
2-3 Tbs oil
chives, chopped

Mix vinegar, wine and pepper with the water and pour over the asparagus. When the liquid has cooled, pour the oil over the asparagus and let it draw well, for at least 1 hour. Sprinkle with the chives just before serving.

Comfrey Salad (Scorzonera hispanica)

2 lbs comfrey

salted water with
1 Tbs vinegar

Wearing rubber gloves and using lukewarm water, remove the sand sticking to the comfrey roots. Peel the roots thinly and place immediately into a mixture of water, vinegar, and flour to prevent discoloring. In a large saucepan filled with a mixture of salted water and 1 Tbs vinegar to cover, boil the comfrey roots for approx. 25-30 minutes. Drain and arrange them on a platter, and use the same dressing as for Asparagus Salad, above. Delicious!

Hop Sprout Salad (Humulus lupulus)

2 lbs hop sprouts
2 cups cooking liquid
1/4 cup light vinegar
white pepper
salt
3 Tbs oil
parsley, chopped

Rub the hop sprouts with coarse salt between your hands. Wash the sprouts. In a large saucepan, boil the sprouts approx. 10 minutes in salted water. Drain, and place in salad bowl. Mix the hot cooking liquid, vinegar and pepper and pour over hop sprouts. Let cool. Add the oil and mix well. Sprinkle with parsley. Let draw well (at least 1 hour).

Beetroot Salad (Beta vulgáris L.)

Beetroot salad is very healthy. Use small beets for best results.
Carefully remove the leaves so as not to make the beets bleed
Since the salad will keep in the refrigerator for a week,it is a
good idea to make a large batch at a time.

2-3 lbs beetroots	Using a vegetable brush,clean the beetroots thoroughly.Put in cold water in a potato steamer,bring to a boil,turn the heat to a low setting and simmer for approx.1 hour (or,in a pressure cooker,for 15-20 minutes). Peel and slice the beets.
3 cups water 1 cup wine vinegar 1 stick cinnamon 1 whole clove 2 lumps sugar 1/2 tsp salt	In a saucepan,bring all ingredients to a quick boil and let boil for 10 minutes. Remove the cinnamon stick and clove.Pour the hot liquid over the beetroot slices. Let draw well,for approx. 1 hour.
1 onion 1 Tbs caraway seeds 3 Tbs oil	Add the onion finely chopped and caraway seeds to the salad. When the salad has cooled,add the oil and mix well.

Tomato Salad (Solanum lycopersicum.)

1 lb firm ripe tomatoes	Wash the tomatoes in lukewarm water and slice them,removing the stalk bases.Arrange the tomato slices in a shallow bowl.Sprinkle with the diced onion and chopped herbs.

1 red or white
  onion, diced
1 Tbs parsley
1 Tbs basil leaves
1 Tbs red wine
  vinegar
pinch of sugar
3 Tbs salad oil
	In a cup,beat vinegar,sugar and oil until thoroughly mixed and pour over the tomatoes.Let draw at least 10 minutes before serving.

Stepchildren, that's what times, particulary in Made to stretch with a green was destroyed  **Vegetables** were in earlier simple Bavarian cooking. dark roux, all that was beyond recognition.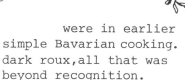
Nowadays people are more nutrition-conscious, they know about vitamins, and this knowledge has brought about a welcome change.

Tender vegetables are steamed or braised only briefly, and mixed with some butter or oil to preserve their individual taste. Another important aspect in preparing vegetables and salads is to choose the right kinds in the right season. "In the summer, eat what grows above the soil, in the winter, eat what grows beneath." (Prof. J. Angerer Munich)

Leaf Spinach

1 1/2 lb spinach
2 Tbs butter or oil
salt & nutmeg, ground

Wash the spinach well and remove the stalks as these contain oxalic acid. Drain very well. Prepare in one of the following ways: Steam the spinach briefly in a small amount of water, drain, add the butter or oil and season with salt and nutmeg to taste; or cook the spinach in batches in a frying pan, using 1 Tbs oil for each batch. Cook rapidly and season to taste.

Buttered Green Beans

1 lb string beans
salted water
1 oz butter or oil
1 shallot, chopped
fresh savory, chopped

Clean the beans, removing the threads, if any, and wash them well. If the beans are too long, break them in half. In an uncovered pot, boil the beans until tender. Do not overcook! Drain the beans and chill them briefly under running cold water, to keep their fresh, green color. In a heatproof pot, heat the butter or oil, add the shallots (optional). Add the beans, shake to coat with the shortening, and only then add the savory (if the savory is cooked with the beans, they lose their individual taste).

Asparagus (Asparagus officinalis L.)

In Bavaria, asparagus counts as a delicacy, since Bavarian asparagus, grown in the Franconian and Swabian territories or in special areas of Old Bavaria, is exceptionally tender. The well-peeled spears may therefore be eaten entirely. Depending on the weather, the asparagus season starts in May -- but it <u>always</u> ends on June 24! The asparagus plant then needs a rest lasting almost a whole year.

Traditional asparagus dishes are: asparagus spears served with melted butter, or asparagus salad served with raw or cooked ham, accompanied by small, new parsley potatoès and young lettuce. What a treat!

There are restaurants in Bavaria which will serve approx. 35 different asparagus dishes in the asparagus season.

Basic Recipe for Asparagus

As a main dish, count 3/4 to 1 lb asparagus per person. As a side dish, count 1/2 lb per person. Use medium thick spears for best results. Thinly peel the asparagus spears, beginning at the tip; let the peel become thicker as you approach the end of the spear. Cut off generously any woody parts. Wash the asparagus and roll it into a kitchen towel moistened with salted water until ready to use.

Half fill a large saucepan with water, add salt to taste, a pinch of sugar and 1 tsp butter and bring to a boil. Add the asparagus. The water should be enough just to cover the asparagus. Cook approx. 20-30 minutes until just done. Do not overcook! It is not necessary to tie the asparagus in bundles: they will cook more uniformly if loose and will not be damaged by the thread.

Buttered Asparagus

3 lbs asparagus spears
chives, chopped
3 1/2 oz. butter, melted

Boil the asparagus (p. 94). Drain, preserving the cooking liquid (which may be used as a soup base). Arrange the asparagus spears on a pre-heated platter. Sprinkle with chives, to taste. Serve with a bowl of melted butter, or heat the butter and pour over the asparagus.

Variations :

2 Tbs parsley
1 tsp dill
1/2 tsp tarragon

Add to the melted butter:

all very finely chopped

- or -

2 Tbs walnut meat, coarsely chopped.

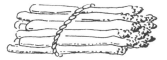

Sauces to Serve with Asparagus

You may serve the following sauces with asparagus spears:

Maltese Sauce

2 egg yolks
2 Tbs ice-cold water
1 Tbs orange juice
pinch of salt

Put the egg yolks, water, orange juice and salt into a heatproof dish, place the dish in a pot of hot water and beat until foamy.

5 oz. butter, melted
1 blood orange
   (untreated)

Gradually add the melted butter, stirring to incorporate. Add the juice and grated rind of an orange. Beat thoroughly, until well mixed. Serve with asparagus spears.

Herb Sauce

1 cup yoghurt
1 Tbs mayonnaise
1 Tbs onion, chopped
1 Tbs parsley, chopped
1 tsp lovage, chopped
1 tsp lemon verbena, chopped
1 Tbs chives, chopped

Beat together all ingredients until well mixed. Serve with asparagus spears.

Mushrooms in Sour Cream

1 1/2-2 lbs mushrooms
4 Tbs butter
1 onion, peeled, but
left whole
1/2 cup heavy cream
1/2 cup sour cream
salt & a little
pepper
1 tsp vinegar
1 Tbs parsley,
chopped

(Boletus edulis Fr.)

There was a time in Old Bavaria, when the only mushroom considered worthy of eating was the yellow boletus, with perhaps a couple of "redcaps" (a local variety) added. Nowadays, an excellent mushroom dish may be prepared from mixed mushrooms, e.g., yellow and chestnut boletus, chanterelles, etc. Clean and, if necessary, briefly wash the mushrooms, drain them very well and finely slice them. In a saucepan heat the butter, add the mushrooms, stir, add the onion, cover and braise 20 minutes, stirring occasionally. After 15 minutes, stir in the heavy and sour cream, and add salt and pepper to taste. Mix in the vinegar and parsley just before serving. IMPORTANT: Add the spices at the end only! Never drink a "Schnaps" after eating mushrooms! "Semmelknödel" (p. 112) are the right things to serve with mushrooms.

Chanterelles with Eggs Reherl mit Ei

2 lbs chanterelles
1 onion, finely
chopped
3 Tbs butter or oil
salt and pepper
4 eggs beaten
together with:
1/2 cup sour cream
2 Tbs parsley,
chopped

Clean the chanterelles well; if necessary, wash them briefly and drain very well. In a frying pan sauté the onions in the butter until glassy. Add the chanterelles and stir them well at high heat (otherwise they will give off too much liquid). Cooking time is approx. 15-20 minutes. After 10 minutes, add salt and fresly ground pepper to taste, mix, then add the eggs-and-cream mixture, and let it set, stirring occasionally. Serve sprinkled with parsley.

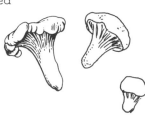

Chanterelles in Cream Sauce

Chanterelles are prepared in the same way as mushrooms (p. 96), but instead of adding the onion uncut, it should be finely chopped and sautéed. Serve with fresh chopped basil leaves.

Brussels Sprouts

Until some years ago Brussels sprouts were invariably served in a light roux. Nowadays they may be prepared in other ways. They taste best when frozen through in the garden and freshly picked.

1 1/2 lbs Brussels sprouts
salted water

3 Tbs butter or oil

parsley, chopped
nutmeg, ground

Clean the sprouts, remove the outer leaves and cut a cross in the stalks. Wash in salted water. Cook in salted water until just tender, but do not overcook! In a heatproof dish, warm the butter or oil, add the well-drained sprouts, and shake to coat them with the shortening. Season with parsley and some nutmeg to taste. You might also try sprinkling 3-4 Tbs stale breadcrumbs into the shortening, frying them, and then adding the Brussels sprouts.

Recipe from Rosa 1888

Red Cabbage

1 1/2-2 lbs red cabbage

vinegar

4 Tbs oil
1-2 apples, chopped
1 large onion, studded with
3 whole cloves
1 lump sugar
1-2 cups broth, or
1-2 cups water

Remove outer leaves of cabbage, quarter it and cut out the stalk. With a vegetable slicer or by hand, cut the cabbage into strips. Sprinkle with vinegar to maintain the color. In a heavy saucepan, heat the oil, add the cabbage and mix in the chopped apples. Bury the clove-studded onion in the cabbage together with the lump of sugar. Add some broth or water, and simmer, covered, for approx. 30-50 minutes, adding more liquid as needed.

Raw Sauerkraut

Raw Sauerkraut is good for your health. In a small bowl, mix some Sauerkraut with 1 Tbs oil and some chopped onion and eat it before a meal.

Sauerkraut I
Upper Bavarian recipe

1 onion, chopped
3 Tbs oil or fat
1 1/2 lbs Sauerkraut
1 apple

2 cups hot broth

In a saucepan, sauté the onion in the oil or fat until it is light yellow and glassy, and add the Sauerkraut, loosened up with a fork. Cut the apple (peeled or unpeeled) into small pieces, add them to the Sauerkraut together with the hot broth, and let it all simmer gently for 1/2 hour. As meat usually takes longer to cook than Sauerkraut, it is advisable to cook it separately and add it to the Sauerkraut only before serving.

Sauerkraut II

Franconian recipe

1 1/2 lbs Sauerkraut
water
pork bones
juniper berries,
   to taste

Rinse the Sauerkraut briefly and put it in a saucepan with some cold water. Add a few pork bones and juniper berries to taste, and simmer until just done. Sauerkraut should never be too soft.

Wine-Kraut

1 Tbs sugar
3 Tbs oil
1 1/2 lbs Sauerkraut
1 cup water or broth
1 cup dry white wine

1/4 lb light grapes

In a saucepan, lightly brown the sugar in the oil, and add the Sauerkraut, loosened up with a fork. Add the water or broth and the wine, cover, and steam gently 1/2 hour. Just before serving, add the grapes. (They are particularly delicate if peeled!)

Bavarian Cabbage Old Bavarian recipe

1 cabbage,approx.
1 1/2 lb
3-4 Tbs oil
1 tsp sugar
2 cups broth
salt,caraway seed

Choose a cabbage that is still nice and
green.Quarter it,remove the stalk,wash it in
salted water and cut it to approx.1 in.
pieces.Do not use a vegetable slicer,unless
you are in a real hurry.In a low-sided saucepan heat the oil,brown the sugar in it,and
add the cabbage.Mix well,add the broth,
season with salt and caraway seed to taste,
cover,and braise the cabbage 40-50 minutes,
until done.
Do not overcook!

Quick White Cabbage Serves 2 persons

approx.1 lb
cabbage head
4 Tbs oil
salt
parsley,chopped
lovage,chopped

Choose a nice,fresh,green head of cabbage.
Quarter it,remove the stalk,wash it in
salted water and cut it into thin slices
(noodles).In a large frying pan heat the oil,
add the cabbage,and cook it rapidly,without
a lid,turning it frequently.Add salt,pars-
ley,and lovage to taste,and serve.

Grated Turnips *Rübenkraut*

You can get them already grated at Bavarian markets

1 1/2 oz.cooking
fat
1 Tbs sugar
1 Tbs onion,
chopped
2 lbs grated
turnips
1-2 cups broth
1-2 Tbs flour
(optional)

In a tall pot,heat the fat,and add the sugar,browning it lightly.Add the chopped
onion and the grated turnips,stir,add the
broth,and let the mixture simmer for 1/2
hour.Test the turnips once in a while to
avoid overcooking. Optional: the sauce may
be thickened with flour (make a smooth
paste of the flour and a small amount of
water,thin it with some of the hot sauce,
return the mixture to the pot and simmer
for a while to remove the floury taste).

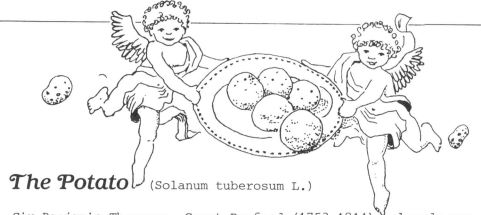

The Potato (Solanum tuberosum L.)

Sir Benjamin Thompson, Count Rumford (1753-1814), already mentioned in another chapter, introduced the potato into Bavaria. Let us be thankful -- after all, what would Bavarian cooking be without the potato?! Although in those times vitamins, mineral values and joules were unknown, the Bavarian housewife did the right thing instinctively by boiling the potatoes in their jackets (skin) and thus preserving the values hidden right underneath the skin. Potatoes cooked in their jackets form the basis of a large number of delicious recipes.

Potatoes Cooked in Their Jackets

Potatoes are best cooked in a potato steamer or in a 4 qt double boiler. They should never be directly in the water. Choose only potatoes without sprouts or green parts, as these contain solanin and are damaging to your health.

1 1/2 lbs potatoes

Wash the potatoes, brush them if necessary, and put them in the top part of the double boiler or the slotted part of the potato steamer. Add water to reach just below the bottom of the inset. Cover and steam the potatoes 25-50 minutes (depending on the age and type of potato). In a pressure cooker, steam the potatoes approx. 6 minutes. Always peel the potatoes while still hot and serve them immediately, or proceed with the various recipes as described therein.

A very good, simple evening meal may consist of new potatoes, boiled, served with butter and with cream cheese mixed with herbs.

He who likes to work a lot and to eat potatoes, can spend many happy hours in Franconia. (Franconian proverb).

Parsley Potatoes

1 1/2 lbs new potatoes
1 oz. butter
1/4 tsp salt
2 Tbs fresh parsley,
   finely chopped

Preferably choose small potatoes. Brush the potatoes and, in a potato steamer or a double boiler, steam them for 20-30 minutes. Peel the potatoes while still hot. In a heatproof dish, heat the butter, add the hot potatoes, sprinkle with salt and parsley, shake to coat and serve immediately.

Creamed Parsley Potatoes (Franconian)

1 1/2 lb salad-type
   potatoes
1 1/2 oz. butter
1 Tbs oil
1 1/2 oz. flour
1 cup cold milk
1 1/2 cups hot meat stock

salt
white pepper, ground
4 Tbs sour cream
1 Tbs light vinegar
4 Tbs parsley, chopped

Boil the potatoes in their jackets. Peel them while still hot and keep them warm. In a saucepan, heat the butter and oil, add the flour, stir in the milk to a smooth consistency, add the hot meat stock and stir to ensure that there are no lumps. Simmer the mixture 15 minutes over low heat. Slice the potatoes and mix them into the sauce. Season with salt and pepper, add the sour cream and vinegar. Just before serving, mix the chopped parsley into the creamed potatoes.

Sawdust Potatoes (Recipe from the Rhön region)

1 1/2 lb small potatoes
2 oz. butter or oil
4-5 Tbs stale breadcrumbs
salt to taste

Boil the potatoes in their jackets, and peel them while still hot. Heat the shortening in a frying pan, add the breadcrumbs, and toast them to a golden brown color. Sprinkle the potatoes with salt, and coat them with the toasted breadcrumbs.

Sour Creamed Potatoes (A genuine Lower Bavarian dish)

4 cups meat stock
2 onions,sliced
3 whole cloves
2 bay leaves
4 juniper berries
salt to taste
3-4 Tbs red wine
vinegar

In a large saucepan, bring all
ingredients to a boil and simmer
for approx. 10 minutes.

1 1/2 lb potatoes
1 oz. butter
2 Tbs oil
1 tsp sugar
1 dill pickle
1 Tbs capers

Boil the potatoes in their jackets. Peel
while still hot, and keep warm.
Heat up the shortening in a heavy skillet,
add the sugar, and brown to a dark golden
color (it will turn bitter if too dark).
Add the flour and toast it,stirring,until
golden brown. Slowly add the strained meat
stock (approx. 3 cups).Simmer 15-20 minutes over low heat.Slice the warm potatoes
and add to liquid. Add the chopped pickle
and capers to taste.

from
Hermine
Antoni

Mashed Peas

1 lb yellow peas
1 oz. butter
1 oz. flour
salt

In a pot, cover the hulled peas with water
and let them soak overnight.Using the same
water,boil the peas until tender.Use no
salt! Make a roux of the butter and flour,
gradually add the pea water, mixing well
to dissolve any knots, bring to a boil and
simmer 15 minutes,stirring occasionally.
Add the peas, and bring to a brief boil.
Pass the mixture through a sieve, and then
add salt to taste. Served with Sauerkraut
and smoked meat, mashed peas are a
Bavarian specialty. They are very filling!

Sautéed Potatoes

1 1/2 lbs salad
(not mealy) potatoes
5-6 Tbs oil or fat
1 onion, thinly
sliced
salt and caraway
seed

Boil the potatoes in their jackets, let them cool, and slice them. In a heavy frying pan, heat the oil or fat, add the onion rings and potato slices, sprinkle with salt and caraway seed, and brown them, turning them a few times. Serve very hot.

Boiled Potatoes

1 lb potatoes
1/2 tsp salt
butter
parsley,
chopped

Choose potatoes that are mealy but remain firm when cooked. Peel the potatoes very thinly, wash them thoroughly, and quarter them. In a pot add water to barely cover the potatoes, add salt and some butter (optional), and simmer the potatoes approx. 20 minutes. Drain off the water, shake the pot, and let the potatoes stand for a few minutes until the steam subsides. Sprinkle with parsley, and serve above all with fish. These potatoes are also suitable for making mashed potatoes.

Mashed Potatoes Franconian recipe

2 lbs mealy potatoes
2 cups milk (level)
salt
nutmeg, ground
1-2 Tbs butter

Prepare the potatoes following the basic recipe for boiled potatoes, above. Drain the potatoes and pass them while still hot through a potato masher into a fireproof dish. In a small saucepan, bring the milk to a boil and beat the boiling milk into the mashed potatoes with an egg beater. Add the salt and nutmeg. Just before serving, mix the butter into the mashed potatoes.

Mashed potatoes may also be prepared with potatoes boiled in their jackets.

Potato Dumplings

Follow these instructions for the preparation of any of the recipes for raw potato dumplings:

Using a potato peeler, very thinly peel 5 lbs mealy potatoes.Wash them well. Then,either place the potatoes in water to which you have added some vinegar,or sulphurate them, to keep their white color. To sulphurate: place the peeled potatoes in a pot,put a 1 in. strip of sulphur on a metal lid (the lid of a jam jar will serve nicely), place this on top of the potatoes and light the sulphur. Immediately put the lid tightly on the pot. The potatoes will be ready for further processing in 5 minutes. They may be grated right away into a large bowl. If you have not fumigated the potatoes but placed them in a water-and-vinegar mixture,drain them well before grating.(According to Prof.F. Flury of Würzburg,sulphurated potatoes are not damaging to your health.)

The potato gratings should not be too "short" but longish. Place the grated potatoes in a "potato sack" over a bowl and press firmly to extract the juice. Put the pressed-out potatoes into a china, glass, or stoneware bowl and add the starch from the potato water as called for in the various recipes. Use a large pot when cooking the potato dumplings to allow them to "swim".

Our Special Potato Dumplings

Prepare the potatoes following the recipe above, but do not add the starch as yet.

4-5 medium-sized, mealy potatoes
water and salt

Thinly peel the potatoes and boil them in salted water until done. Remove the potatoes. Add the starch from the pressed-out raw potatoes to the hot potato broth,bring to a boil, and cook it to a mush. Pass the boiled potatoes through a potato masher, add them, together with the starch,to the prepared raw potato dough, add salt to taste, and shape the dough into dumplings of approx. 3 in. dia. Simmer in salted water approx. 3/4 hour.

Potato Dumplings

5 lbs potatoes, raw
1 lb boiled potatoes
(yesterday's)
1 cup plain yoghurt or
1 cup "gestöckelte"
milk p.168
1 tsp salt

Prepare the raw potatoes as described in the recipe on p. 104. Grate the boiled potatoes and add them to the raw ones. Add the yoghurt or "gestöckelte" milk and the salt, and mix. Shape the dough into dumplings and simmer them in salted water for 40 minutes.

Raw "Klöss"

In Lower Franconia, these dumplings are called simply "Klöss". Prepare the potatoes as described on p. 104.

2 buns (yesterday's)
3 Tbs oil or butter
2 cups boiling milk
approx. 2 1/2 oz.
coarse semolina
1/2 tsp salt

Finely dice the buns, and toast them in the oil or butter to a light brown color. Put aside. - Pour half of the milk over the pressed-out potatoes. With the other half, semolina and salt, prepare a thick sauce and put it, hot, over the potatoes. Add the potato starch remaining in the potato water. Mix all ingredients, and shape the dough into dumplings. Stick a cube of toasted bread in the center of each dumpling and re-shape. Put the dumplings into boiling salted water, return the water to a boil until they start floating, partially uncover, turn the heat down and let the "Klöss" simmer 30 minutes. Serve immediately.

"Robber Dumplings"

They were dark as storm clouds just before a cloudburst because they were not sulphurated -- and their texture was so beautiful that it would be a pity to let the old recipe fade into the past. Here goes: Top the pressed-out potatoes, to which you have added the starch (see recipe p.104) with the following:
2 stale buns, very finely sliced
1 ladleful "gestöckelte" milk or yoghurt (1 small cup), and some salt. Knead the dough well, and shape into smallish dumplings of approx. 2 in. dia. Let the dumplings simmer gently for 3/4 hour in salted water.

"Silky" Potato Dumplings

from Aunt Herta Würzburg.

2 1/2 lbs potatoes
(boiled the day
before in their
jackets)
9 oz. potato flour
2 cups water,
boiling hot
1 tsp salt
salted water,
butter or oil
white bread, diced

Peel the potatoes and grate them into a
bowl. Add the potato flour, mix, then add
the hot water and salt, and knead the mixture quickly into a dough. Form the dough
into dumplings, and let the dumplings simmer in boiling salted water for 12-15 minutes. (The dumplings may be left longer
in the water, they will not turn dark.)
Optional: try stuffing the dumplings with
diced white bread toasted in butter or
oil.

from Ellen Stumpf.

Small Potato Dumplings

3 lbs mealy potatoes
(boiled the day before)
1/4 lb butter
3 eggs
salt
4 Tbs flour
4 Tbs stale
breadcrumbs
1 1/2 oz. butter

Peel and grate the potatoes. In a bowl,
stir the butter vigorously until foamy.
Add the eggs and salt, mix well, add the
grated potatoes, and work the mixture
into a dough with a cooking spoon. Form
small (1 1/2 in.) dumplings and simmer
them 25 minutes in salted water. Toast
the breadcrumbs in the butter and
sprinkle over the drained dumplings.

Toasted Potato Dumplings from Franconia

This dish is prepared with leftover potato dumplings.

Potato Dumplings
oil

Slice the potato dumplings. Heat up some
oil in a frying pan and toast the dumpling slices on both sides until golden
and crisp. Serve with a salad.

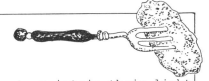

Potato Pancakes   Reiberdatschi

2 3/4 lbs mealy
potatoes,peeled

1 tsp salt
oil for frying

Sulphurate the potatoes to maintain their light
color (optional;see Dumplings, p.104). Grate
the raw potatoes through the large holes of
a grater,making long flakes.Drain off some of
the juice,add salt and mix well.With a tablespoon,form 3 in.dia.patties.Fry in hot oil
until edges turn brown (up to that point the
pancakes will stick to the pan!),turn and fry
until crisp.Keep in a warm oven until serving,
or serve the pancakes in portions as you bake
them. Serve with apple sauce or,if preferred,with cucumber salad.

Potato Pancakes   Franconian Recipe

2 3/4 lbs mealy
potatoes,peeled
1 tsp salt
1-2 eggs
appr.3 Tbs flour
oil for frying

Prepare the potatoes as described above.Add
the egg(s) and flour.Proceed as described
above,but make slightly thicker patties.In
Franconia,these pancakes are eaten with
lingonberry (cranberry) preserve.

Potato Noodles   Ritschinudeln

Recipe from the
Bavarian Forest

2 3/4 lbs mealy
potatoes,peeled
2 Tbs thick sour
cream
1 bun,at least
one day old
1 tsp salt
1 1/2 oz.
clarified
butter,or oil
2 eggs
1 cup sour cream

Coarsely grate the potatoes.In a "potato
sack" or linen cloth,press the gratings to
extract the moisture.Save the liquid, and
add the settled starch to the dough. Slice
the bun very thinly and add to the potatoes
with the sour cream and salt.Mix well,knead
to a dough,and make noodles of finger thick-
ness.Simmer the noodles gently 15-20 minutes
in salted water.Drain well.In a roasting pan,
heat the shortening.Add the noodles. In a
preheated 480° F oven,lightly roast the noodles,shaking the pan once in a while.
Just before serving,mix the eggs,cream and
milk,pour over the noodles,and let the mixture thicken and settle. Serve with cabbage
or lettuce.

Potato Dough Basic Recipe

2 lbs mealy potatoes

Boil the potatoes in their jackets, peel them while still hot und press the hot potatoes through a potato masher. An even better procedure is to boil the potatoes the day before using and to grate them, cold, through a grater with large holes, letting them flake loosely and flatly onto a pastry board.

2 1/2 oz. flour
1 tsp salt
1 egg
1 egg yolk

Sprinkle the flour over the potatoes, add the salt, egg and egg yolk, and knead it all rapidly and loosely to a dough. Do not press! Proceed immediately with recipe, as prescribed.

Potato Noodles

Prepare a potato dough, using potatoes boiled the day before and grated, as described above. Form a roll. Cut off slices and roll them into noodles the thickness of a finger. In a heavy skillet or frying pan, heat clarified butter, add the noodles and fry them all over until they turn golden brown. Serve immediately.

Potato Dollars

Prepare a potato dough as described under Potato Noodles. Form a roll 2 in. thick and cut off pieces 1/4 in. thick from the roll. In a heavy skillet or frying pan, fry the potato dollars in clarified butter or vegetable oil on both sides until golden brown. Serve immediately.

Regensburg Stritzeln

This is an adaptation of the old recipe,
dating back to 1866, of the famous Maria
Schandri. There is an old Stritzel bakery
in a narrow side street in the oldest part of Regensburg. Na-
tives of Regensburg still love their Stritzel soup, as do all
visitors. When making Stritzeln they should be fried in clarified butter that has already been used in frying other dough;
with this method the Stritzeln will acquire their typical taste.

1 1/4 pound flour
4 whole eggs
1/4 tsp salt
1 cup milk
clarified butter

Sift the flour onto a pastry board and form a
well in the center. In a deep bowl, mix well
the eggs, salt, and 12 egg-shells'full (i.e.
1 cup) milk. Gradually mix this mixture into
the flour with the help of a knife. In a wide,
deep pan, or a shallow fireproof dish, melt
enough clarified butter to come up halfway on the sides. Cut off
strips from the dough (about the size of a finger). With well -
floured hands, shape the soft strips slightly and lay them carefully into the pan, alongside one another, until they cover the
bottom. Heat the pan and baste the strips steadily with the fat
until they are browned. Drain the strips in a sieve and serve
them in soup (see p.30)

Cottage Cheese Noodles Ziegernudle

1/2 lb flour
1 1/2 lbs cottage cheese
(dry Topfen)
1 egg
pinch of salt
1 Tbs sour cream
clarified butter
2 1/2 oz. sugar
(optional)

Sift the flour onto a pastry board and add the Topfen, pressing it through a potato masher. Add the egg, salt, and sour cream, and knead it all rapidly to a dough. Shape rolls the thickness of your thumb, and cut them into 2 1/2 in. pieces. In a frying pan heat the butter and fry the "noodles" to a golden yellow color. Serve them with Sauerkraut. Optional: If you prefer them sweet, add sugar to the dough, and serve the sweet "noodles" with stewed fruit.

Potato Noodles Bauchstecherl

Prepare a raw potato dough (p.104), but use only 2 lbs potatoes. Then:

1 1/2 lbs potatoes,
boiled in their skins
3 Tbs flour
1 tsp salt
salted water
2 oz. clarified butter
or oil
3 eggs
1/2 cup milk or cream

Boil the potatoes in their skins, then peel them and pass them, hot, through a potato masher. Add them to the raw potato dough to which you have also added the starch, add the flour and salt, and knead it all rapidly to a dough. Form the dough into a roll approx. 2 1/4 in. thick, cut off thick slices and form these into 3 in. "noodles". Boil the noodles 12–15 minutes in salted water (you may have to do this in batches if the pot is not large enough, as the "noodles" will stick if the pot is too small). Drain the noodles well. In a roasting pan in a preheated 420° F oven, heat the butter or oil, add the "noodles", and brown them, shaking or turning them

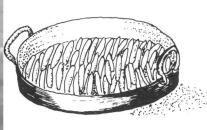

several times. Sauerkraut or red cabbage go nicely with this dish. Optional: If you want a more substantial meal, mix the eggs with the milk or cream, pour over the noodles in the pan, and let the mixture set in the oven before serving.

Bread Dumplings   Semmelknödel

10 stale white buns
or 1 lb stale white
bread
2 cups boiling milk
1 large onion,
finely chopped
1 oz. butter
3 Tbs parsley, finely
chopped
1 lemon, untreated
1/2 tsp salt
3 eggs

Use plain buns without caraway or poppy
seeds. Cut the buns or bread into very
thin small slices. In a bowl, pour the
boiling milk over the bread, mix, and let
stand for at least 1 hour. Sauté the
onion in the butter until glassy, add the
parsley and the finely chopped rind of
the lemon, and add the mixture to the
bread. Season with salt, add the eggs, and
mix well. Wetting your hands, form a
"trial" dumpling of approx. 2 1/2 in. dia.
In a large pot (holding approx. 7 qts)
bring plenty of salted water to a boil,
and try cooking the dumpling in it. If
it stays intact and loses none of its
substance, add the remaining dumplings.
(Should the "trial" dumpling be un-
satisfactory, add some flour to the dough.) Bring the water to
the boil again: when the dumplings start swimming on top of the
water, reduce the heat and let the dumplings simmer gently for
20 minutes, with the pot only half covered. Remove them with a
slotted spoon and lightly shake off the water.

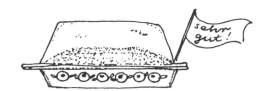

Baked Dumpling

Prepare a "Knödel" dough as described above and place it in a buttered heatproof dish. Dot with butter flakes, cover, and bake in
a preheated 420°F oven for approx. 1/2 hour. The dough should
have a light brown, thin crust; you may want to leave it uncovered for the last 10 minutes baking time. Serve in the heatproof
dish.

Dumplings in Calf's Caul

This is an almost forgotten old Bavarian specialty. It is an excellent accompaniment to stuffed veal breast, roast veal, or roast chicken.

1 calf's caul (great omentum)
bread dumpling dough (p. 112) from:
1/2 lb buns or white bread
1/2 cup milk
2 whole eggs
1 egg yolk

Wash the calf's caul well in salted water. Dry and spread it apart. Cut off any thick edges.
Prepare a bread dumpling dough from these ingredients and season with the customary spices.

Place the dough into the spread calf's caul, fold the ends over the filling, roll it up and fasten it with a heavy thread or cord (a thin thread would cut the caul!). Place the roll alongside the meat in the roasting pan and roast it along with the meat. Cut into slices to serve.

Toasted Dumplings

Leftover "Semmelknödel" (Bread Dumplings) may be turned to good use as a small lunch or supper dish.

Leftover Semmelknödel (cold)
butter
2 eggs
1/4 cup milk
salt - or -
sugar and cinnamon

Cut the Semmelknödel into 1/8 in. slices. In a frying pan, heat up the butter and toast the "Knödel" slices on both sides. In a cup, mix the eggs with the milk, pour the mixture over the toasted Knödel slices and let it set. Salt lightly, and serve with a salad, or sprinkle with sugar and cinnamon and serve with stewed fruit.

Dumpling Salad   Old Bavarian Recipe

Leftover Semmelknödel (cold)
1/2 cup watered-down vinegar
1 onion, sliced
2 Tbs vegetable oil

Cut up the leftover Semmelknödel (Bread Dumplings) into 1/8 in. slices. Douse with the vinegar. Add the onion. Mix well, and let draw for at least 1 hour. Add the oil and mix again.

"Spätzle"

"Spätzle" are prepared in many different shapes:
there is the round button-shaped variety where the
dough is stirred through the holes of a Spätzle
sieve, or the oblong,Swabian kind,where the Spätzle are cut with
a scraping motion from a board,or are made with the help of a
Spätzle slicer or press.Spätzle prepared with milk only will be
firmer.Loose,tender Spätzle are made the following way:

1 lb flour
1/2 cup milk
1 cup soda water
4 whole eggs
1 tsp salt
butter

Sift the flour into a bowl,and add the milk
and soda water,mixing well. Add the eggs and
salt,mix,and beat the dough with a wooden
spoon until small bubbles form. Let the
dough rest for 1/2 hour.In the meantime,boil
up plenty of salted water in a large pot.
Cut or slice the "Spätzle" in batches into
the boiling water,bring each batch briefly
to a boil,then lift out with a slotted spoon,
drain in a colander and chill under running
cold water.Spread the Spätzle on a board to
steam off the moisture,then heat them in
butter before serving.

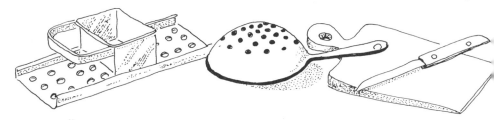

Cheese "Spätzle"

Prepare "Spätzle" as described above.After boiling,immediately
douse them with running <u>hot</u> water,and shake them well in a colander,to remove the water.In a preheated dish,mix the Spätzle
with 2 oz.butter and 6 oz.freshly grated Swiss cheese.Place the
dish in the warm oven until all Spätzle have been cooked and
added.Optional: top the Cheese Spätzle with sautéed onion rings.
Serve with lettuce.

Pasta Dough

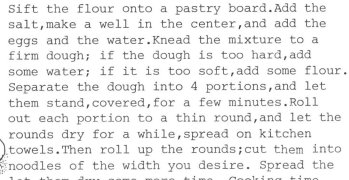

1 lb flour
1 Tbs salt
4 whole eggs
4 eggshells' full
water

Sift the flour onto a pastry board.Add the salt,make a well in the center,and add the eggs and the water.Knead the mixture to a firm dough; if the dough is too hard,add some water; if it is too soft,add some flour. Separate the dough into 4 portions,and let them stand,covered,for a few minutes.Roll out each portion to a thin round,and let the rounds dry for a while,spread on kitchen towels.Then roll up the rounds;cut them into noodles of the width you desire. Spread the noodles loosely and let them dry some more time. Cooking time for these noodles is approx.10 minutes for broad noodles, approx. 5 minutes for soup noodles, and approx. 8 minutes for small squares.

Ham and Noodles

Prepare a noodle dough as described above.Cut broad noodles approx. 1/3 in.wide. Cook the noodles in plenty of boiling salted water,drain,and douse them with hot water. In a frying pan,melt the butter,add the noodles,mix,then add the ham and

1 1/2 oz. butter
1/2 lb cooked ham,
finely diced
1/4 lb Swiss cheese,
freshly grated

cheese and mix loosely.Serve hot,with a mixed salad.

Ham and Patches

Prepare a noodle dough as described above.Cut strips approx. 3/4 in.wide, then cut the strips crosswise to obtain small squares (patches). Cook the patches in boiling salted water approx.6-8 minutes until "al dente". Do not overcook! Drain, chill under running cold water,and drain again.In a large

1/2 lb cooked ham,
finely diced
1 1/2 oz.butter

frying pan,melt the butter,add the noodle patches and the diced ham and mix loosely but thoroughly. Serve with lettuce,to make a light meal.

Swabian Meat Pouches

From Aunt Nini, Kempten

Prepare a pasta dough, p. 115, using 1/2 lb flour, 2 eggs, 1/2 tsp salt and 5 Tbs water. Roll out the dough 1/8 in. thick and cut it into 5x5 in. squares.

1 lb smoked, cooked meat

5 Tbs green onion stalks, cut in thin rings

1 white bun, finely diced

1 pancake, cut in fine strips

1 egg white

salted water

Dice the meat very finely, or put it through a meat grinder. Mix the meat, onion rings, diced bun and pancake strips and put a spoonful of the mixture in the center of each square of dough. Brush the edges of the squares with the lightly beaten egg white, and fold them into triangles, pressing down the edges to seal. Place the triangles carefully into boiling salted water and let them draw, simmering, for 5 minutes. Remove and drain the triangles. Use them either in a "Meat Pouch Soup" ("Maultaschen-suppe"), or make them into the following dish:

Meat Pouches in Butter

A Recipe from the Allgäu region

Prepare the meat pouches as described above. Coat the bottom of a heatproof casserole with 1 Tbs butter and arrange a layer of meat pouches to cover the bottom of the dish. Sprinkle with 2 Tbs grated cheese. Continue the layers of butter, meat pouches, and cheese; the top layer should be cheese. Put in a preheated 420°F oven and leave until the cheese has melted.

Butter, melted

Swiss cheese, grated

A tip: Use fresh Swiss cheese if you want the cheese to draw threads when melted. Incidentally: grated cheese will keep for a long time in your freezer.

"Shoved Noodles"

1 lb flour
1 tsp salt
1 1/2 cups water
salted water
residue from
clarified butter
- or -
lard

Sift the flour onto a pastry board, add the salt and 1 1/2 cups water and work it into a dough. Shape the dough into a roll, cut off thin slices, and roll ("shove") the slices into small sausage-shaped noodles. Let them dry a few minutes, then boil them gently in salted water for 5 minutes. Remove, drain, and chill them under cold water, then drain them well. In a large frying pan heat either some residue left over from clarifying butter, or lard, to cover the bottom of the pan, add the noodles, and fry them, turning them with a spatula, to a nice golden brown color. Serve them mixed with Sauerkraut (p.98), or "sweet cabbage", i.e., Bavarian Cabbage (p.99). Optional: top with sautéed onion rings.

Swabian Cabbage Doughnuts

1 small onion,
finely chopped
1 Tbs oil
2 1/2 oz. smoked bacon,
finely diced
1/2 lb Sauerkraut
1 small apple,
unpeeled, chopped

Prepare a pasta dough (p. 115). Fry the onion in the oil, together with the diced bacon. Drain the Sauerkraut and chop it up a little. In a large bowl, mix the Sauerkraut with the bacon mixture and the cored, chopped apple. Roll out half of the pasta dough to 1/6 in. thickness, and mark 2 in. rings with a cookie cutter. Put a small mound of the Sauerkraut mix into the center of each ring. Roll out the second half of the pasta dough, place it on top of the first half, and cut out the filled doughnuts, pressing down the edges to seal.

2 Tbs oil
3 slices bacon
1/2 cup hot broth

In a heavy, wide saucepan, fry the bacon slices in the oil, push them to the side, add the doughnuts, gently add the hot broth, cover, and braise at medium heat for 1/2 hour. The doughnuts are done when they have a brown crust on the underside.

Lentil Soup with "Spätzle"

1/4 lb flour
1/4 cup water
1/2 tsp salt
1 whole egg
8 cups salted water

1 oz. butter
1/2 tsp sugar
3 Tbs flour
1 can lentils (1 lb)
Water or broth
2 oz. smoked, streaky
  bacon, diced
1 Tbs oil

Beat together the flour, water, salt and egg and let the dough stand for 1/2-1 hour. In a large pot, bring the salted water to a boil. Moisten a small cutting board and cut the "Spätzle" (small oblong dumplings) from the board into the water. Heat the water again, and when it has boiled up once again thoroughly, drain the "Spätzle" in a colander, and rinse them in running warm water. Clean the pot quickly, dry it thoroughly, and use it to toast the flour and sugar in the butter to a light brown color. Add the liquid from a can of lentils, beating vigorously to dissolve any lumps and let simmer for 1/4 hour to remove the floury taste. Add some water or broth, if needed, then add the lentils and the "Spätzle". Fry the diced bacon to a golden color and sprinkle it, hot, onto the soup just before serving.

Peasant Treat

2 lbs potatoes
  (firm-cooking)
1/2 lb smoked streaky
  bacon, diced
3 large onions,
  sliced
4 eggs
1/2 cup milk
salt and pepper
  to taste
chives, chopped

Boil the potatoes in their jackets, peel them while still hot, and slice them. In a frying pan, fry the bacon. Pour off the excess bacon fat. Add the onions and potatoes, brown them on one side, turn and brown them on the other side. In a bowl, beat together the eggs and the milk. Pour the mixture over the potatoes in the pan and let it set. Season with salt and pepper and serve in the pan, sprinkled generously with chives. Serve with fresh lettuce. In the Bavarian countryside, instead of the lettuce this dish is served with "gestöckelte" milk (p. 168).

Swabian Tramp Soup

Recipe from a ski châlet
in the Allgäu region

This dish has nothing in common with a soup. Actually, it is
an eating game, played with dice: the person who scores 6 with
the dice may eat until the next score of 6 comes up. Some
people starve, while others just eat, and eat, and eat... It's
lots of fun! Arrange the following on a large platter:

1/2 lb ham, cooked, diced
1/2 lb Swiss cheese from the Allgäu, diced
1/2 lb cold meat, diced
5 sweet-sour pickled gherkins, sliced
4 large onions, sliced
2 Tbs capers
3 apples, washed, unpeeled, diced. Prepare a dressing:

1-1 1/2 cups watered-down
  vinegar
1 Tbs mustard
8 Tbs oil

Mix all ingredients together,
pour over the meats, mix and
let draw well (about 1 hour).

Noodle Salad (Swabian recipe)

Noodle salad may be prepared from home-made or commercially
made noodles. It is a good way to use up leftover noodles.

approx. 1/2 lb noodles
1/2 cup watered-down vinegar
2 Tbs vegetable oil
4 oz. cooked ham, diced
3 oz. Swiss cheese, slivered
chives, chopped

Boil the noodles in salted water
until they have reached an al
dente consistency. Chill them
in cold water and drain well.
Mix the vinegar and oil and
pour the mixture over the
noodles. Add the ham and cheese.
Mix well. Sprinkle with the
chives.

119

Bavarian Pastries and Fasting Dishes

The Catholic Church has given its followers in Bavaria -- who, by the way, constitute almost three-quarters of the state's population -- many feast days and holidays. At the same time she has, however, obliged them to observe a number of days of fasting and abstinence.

Fasting days are those on which only one main meal is permitted, while on days of abstinence no meat may be eaten. To this day, Good Friday and Ash Wednesday remain strict days of fasting and abstinence. Since, in earlier times, every Friday was a day of abstinence, consequently a large number of recipes for main-course pastries - also called fasting dishes, *Fastenspeisen*-were devised.

The main-course pastry dish - called *Mehlspeis*-has a special standing in Bavaria. Preceded by a soup which is preferably made of vegetables, or a fresh, mixed salad, the pastry dish becomes a full meal. It is often accompanied by some stewed fruit, if it has not been made with fruit to begin with.

All Strudels, for example, fall into the Mehlspeis category; a Strudel is also served as a dessert only if the meal preceding it was not a very rich one.

Desserts as we know them today were only familiar at court in earlier times; they were unknown in simple, peasant cooking.

Church rules for fasting and abstinence have been eased — whether this is a blessing from the point of view of health is debatable. The many voluntary diets nowadays seem to indicate that the old periods of fasting, mostly observed in springtime, were not all that out of place, after all.

"Rainworms"

1/2 lb flour
1 egg
1 Tbs cream
pinch of salt
1/4 cup water
4 cups milk,
boiling
3 oz. butter
1 1/2 oz.sugar
vanilla sugar

Sift the flour onto a pastry board. Make a well in the center of the flour and add the egg, cream,salt,and water.Mix it all with a knife, then knead the mixture into a dough.Let the dough rest for 1/2 hour,covered.Then shape it into a roll,cut off thin slices,and roll these to "worms" of the thickness of a pencil.Let the "worms" dry on the board for 1/2 hour,then sim- mer them approx.5 minutes in the milk,and drain. Preheat the oven to 420°F. In a heavy pan, heat the butter,sprinkle it with sugar,add the "rainworms", and bake them,uncovered, to a golden brown color,turning them occasionally. Should they get too dry, add a little boiling milk. They should be moist and have a nice crust.Cooking time is approx.1/2 hour.Sprinkle with vanilla sugar to taste before serving.

"Plucked Bonnets"

Prepare a half-portion yeast dough,following the instructions of the basic recipe (p.123),but using no sugar.After the dough has risen,shape it into a fat roll, cut off slices, and roll these into rounds of approx. 3 in. dia.In a heavy pan (large enough so that the liquid should be approx.1 in.deep) warm up 2 cups milk, 2 cups cream,2 Tbs clarified butter, and 1 Tbs sugar. Quickly arrange the "bonnets" in the pan, cover them well, and cook them at medium heat for approx. 25 minutes.As in the case of steamed doughnuts (Dampfnudeln), it is important that the "bonnets" have nice crusts.Sprinkle with vanilla sugar before serving.

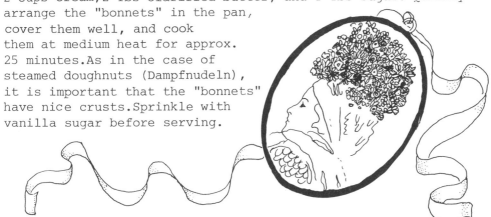

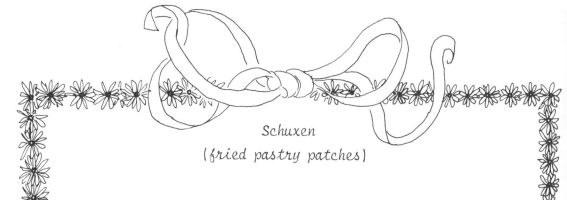

Schuxen
(fried pastry patches)

an old Bavarian recipe by Aunt Mary from Dingolfing.

To make Schuxen, you will need a small cupful of leaven
from the baker's. In a warm bowl, sift together 1/2 lb
wheat flour and 1/2 lb rye flour. Mix the leaven with
some flour and put it into a well in the center of the
wheat and rye flour mound, letting it rise for approx.
15 minutes. Then add 1/4 lb Topfen (dry cottage cheese)
passed through a sieve, and 1/2 cup lukewarm milk. Beat
and knead the dough well until it begins to form bubbles,
then let it rise 1 hour. Roll out the dough into thin,
oblong patches, let it expand once more briefly, and fry
the ovals swimming in fat. They may be served to accompany vegetables, or they may be sprinkled with sugar and
served with stewed fruit.

Yeast Dough Basic Recipe

In every part of Bavaria yeast dough constitutes the basis for a large variety of breads, pastries and cakes. Since yeast is a biological leavener, its use should take preference over the use of chemical leaveners. There is no need to be apprehensive about handling it: if you follow the procedure outlined below, your yeast dough should always be a success:

1. All ingredients should have the same temperature.
2. Salt and fat should never come into direct contact with the yeast.
3. The dough should never be exposed to a draught when it is rising.
4. Prepare a preliminary dough to test the yeast and shorten the rising time.

Here we go:
1 3/4 lbs flour
2 oz. yeast
1 Tbs sugar
3 Tbs lukewarm milk
1/4 lb butter - or margarine
1 Tbs lard - or clarified butter
1/4 lb sugar
1 Tbs vanilla sugar
pinch of salt
1/2 - 1 cup lukewarm milk
2 eggs

Sift the flour into a large, pre-warmed bowl and put in a warm place. Crumble the yeast into a cup and mix it with the sugar and the 3 Tbs milk. Make a hollow in the center of the flour, pour in the yeast mixture and mix a handful of flour with it. Cut the butter and the lard or clarified butter into small pieces and distribute over the flour "ring". Sprinkle sugar, and salt over it all Cover with a clean cloth and let rest for approx. 10 minutes. Using a large headed cooking spoon, beat the mixture first with the flour and then with the 1/2 cup lukewarm milk until bubbles form in the dough. Cover again and let rise for approx. 3/4- 1 hour or until the dough for plaited yeast bread, yeast dumplings, etc.

Yeast Dough Steamed Doughnuts

Called "Dampfnudeln", these doughnuts are a typical Old Bavarian specialty. You may need a little practice to obtain optimal results.

1 lb flour
1 oz. yeast
1 tsp sugar -and
1/2 cup milk
1 1/2 oz. butter
1 1/2 oz. sugar
pinch of salt
2 eggs

Prepare yeast dough as described in basic recipe (p.123)

Into a 1o in. baking dish with a tight-fitting cover, or a covered casserole dish, pour enough warm milk to reach just under 1 in.up the sides.Add 2-3 Tbs butter and 1 Tbs sugar.Using a tablespoon, cut pieces from the dough, form them into balls and place them in the dish, side by side. Let them rise briefly.Cover, and bake them at medium heat on top of the stove approx.1/2 hour, without opening the lid. A heatproof dish with a glass cover will make it easier to observe the process. The doughnuts should "sing", i.e., it should be audible that the milk has been absorbed. Leave the cover on for a while after baking, then jerk it off to prevent the steam from falling back upon the doughnuts and making them collapse. Your effort at curbing your curiosity will be rewarded! The doughnuts will have nice, brown crusts around the bottom, formed of the milk, sugar, and butter. Use a pancake turner to lift them out one by one.

Try this variation: use water instead of milk to obtain firmer crusts.Or leave off all liquid and use de-stoned plums with sugar or sliced apples to completely cover bottom of dish.

"Dampfnudeln" are served with vanilla sauce or vanilla chaudeau (p. 125). Cut leftover Dampfnudeln in slices, coat them with beaten egg, and fry in butter. Serve sprinkled with sugar and cinnamon.

Vanilla Sauce

Home-made vanilla sauce will taste incomparably better than a
ready-made, synthetic product. Just try it!

3 egg yolks
2 Tbs sugar
2 Tbs vanilla sugar
1 Tbs cornstarch
1 1/2 cups milk
1 vanilla bean

Mix the egg yolks, sugar, vanilla sugar
and cornstarch, stirring vigorously until
smooth. Add the milk, beating it in with
a whisk. Slit the vanilla bean lengthwise,
scrape out the seeds, and add the bean and
the seeds to the egg-and-milk mixture. Beat
over mild heat until the sauce begins to
thicken -- do not boil! Remove and discard
the vanilla bean. Serve immediately.

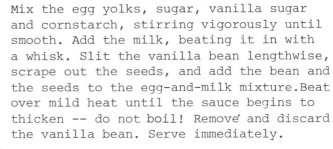

Vanilla Chaudeau

Prepare in the same way as vanilla sauce, but add stiffly beaten
egg whites to the sauce, as follows:

2 egg whites
1/2 tsp lemon juice
1 tsp sugar

Beat all together until the mixture holds
stiff peaks, then fold carefully into the
hot vanilla sauce.

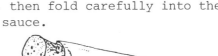

Clear Wine Sauce

2 cups dry white wine
or
2 cups dry red wine
1 cinnamon stick,
approx. 1 in.
approx. 3 Tbs sugar
1/2 lemon, untreated

In a saucepan heat up the wine with the
cinnamon, the sugar (to taste) and the
thin peel of the lemon (without the white
inner rind). Do not boil!

Yeast Dumplings Rohrnudeln

Prepare yeast dough, following the basic recipe on p. 123. Let the dough rise.

3 oz. butter, or
2 1/2 oz. clarified
   butter

confectioner's sugar

Warm the butter carefully in an 8x12 in. baking pan or fireproof dish. Using a tablespoon, cut the dough into 16 even portions. Roll the portions into balls and place them, side by side, into the melted warm butter. Cover the pan and let the dough rise briefly once again. Preheat the oven to 380°F. Brush the dumplings several times with melted butter. Bake them uncovered 30 min. until golden brown. Unmold and separate the dumplings, sprinkle them with sugar, and serve them with a side dish of vanilla sauce. (P.125)

The "Rohrnudeln" may also be eaten cold, and may be deep-frozen.

from Aunt Mary.

Ducat Dumplings

Prepare a yeast dough following the basic recipe on p. 123. After the dough has risen, preheat the oven to 450°F.

3 oz. butter
   - or -
   clarified butter
1/2 cup heavy cream
1/2 cup milk
5 Tbs coarse sugar
5 Tbs nuts, coarsely
   chopped
butter to brush

In a roasting pan, heat up the butter with the cream, milk, sugar and nuts, and mix well. Using a tablespoon, cut plum-sized dumplings from the yeast dough, set them close into the butter mixture in the pan, let them rise once again briefly, and bake them approx. 30 minutes, until golden brown. Brush with melted butter, and serve with warm vanilla sauce, p. 125 , or vanilla chaudeau, p. 125 . Ducat Dumplings are nice when served with coffee. They may also be deep-frozen.

Bavarian Cream

5 leaves gelatine
1 lb raspberries, fresh or frozen
5 oz. sugar
1 Tbs lemon juice
1 cup heavy cream

pistachio nuts
whipped cream

Soak the gelatine in cold water. Purée the raspberries (if using frozen fruit, unfreeze before use) in a blender. (Save a few berries for decoration.) Mix the raspberry purée with the sugar and lemon juice until the sugar is dissolved. Pour 6 Tbs of the mixture into a small saucepan, heat it up and dissolve the squeezed gelatine in it. Add the gelatine mixture to the cold raspberry mixture. Wait until mixture begins to set. Whip the heavy cream until it holds stiff peaks and fold carefully but thoroughly into the raspberry mixture. Transfer the mixture into a serving bowl or individual serving glasses and refrigerate at least 3 hrs. Garnish with whole raspberries, pistachio nuts and dabs of whipped cream. If you wish to unmold the cream, pour it into a mold rinsed with cold water and let it settle, refrigerated, overnight. Unmold and garnish as desired.

Vanilla Cream

2 cups milk
1 vanilla bean
4 eggs
5 1/2 oz. sugar
1 Tbs vanilla sugar
butter (for coating)

Slit the vanilla bean lengthwise, add to the milk, bring to a boil, and let cool. Mix eggs, sugar and vanilla sugar until very thick and foamy. Add the vanilla milk. Spoon the mixture into a well-buttered heatproof dish or 4 large cups, leaving room to spare. Place the dish or cups into a pot of boiling water. (Water should reach no higher than about 7/8 in. below rim.) Simmer 1/2 hour. If a very deep dish is used, place into the oven after 1/2 hour on top, covered with aluminum foil (pricked with a fork so steam can escape) for another 1/4 hour. The surface of the (cooled) dessert should be firm before it is unmolded. Serve with whipped cream and fruit.

Cranberry Cream

2 leaves gelatine
7 oz. cranberries
(preserved)
1 Tbs lemon juice
5 Tbs hot water
1 1/2 cups heavy cream

Soak the gelatine in water 5 minutes. Pass the cranberries through a sieve. Mix with the lemon juice until smooth. Squeeze the gelatine, dissolve it in the hot water, and add it to the fruit. Whip the cream until stiff and fold it into the fruit mixture. Fill into individual glasses; refrigerate at least 2 hrs. Garnish with whipped cream and wafers.

Fine Strawberries

This is a favorite dessert of the Bavarians. The berries (whether wild or garden strawberries) should be ripe. They will keep their taste best if washed in mineral water "Selterswasser". Drain them well, put them in a bowl and prick the larger berries with a fork (cutting them will diminish their taste!). Sprinkle with a few drops lemon juice, sweeten sparingly with sugar, and let the berries draw for a while. Whip the cream until it holds soft peaks and fold it gently into the berries. You might try to mash some of the berries, mixing them with the cream and adding the mixture to the remaining berries; or you might try to pour a small amount of almond liqueur over the berries, for a new, delicious taste.

Raspberry Ice Cream

You can prepare this dessert in a hurry if you have deep-frozen raspberries (or blackberries). This recipe, by the way, has no roots in Granny's cookbook - she had no freezer ! It is, however, a tested and proven favorite in our house.

2 cups heavy cream
10-14 oz. raspberries
(or bilberries)
4 oz. sugar

Whip the cream until it holds soft peaks. Add the frozen raspberries or bilberries, with the (optional) sugar. Mix briefly with an electric mixer, or in a blender, until creamy. Serve immediately. If prepared ahead of serving time, it is best to store the ice cream in the freezing compartment of your refrigerator.

Fine Chocolate Almond Cream

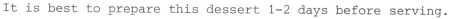

It is best to prepare this dessert 1-2 days before serving.

2 Tbs sugar
3 oz. slivered almonds
10 oz. semi-sweet
chocolate
8 egg whites
1 tsp lemon juice
1 cup heavy cream

Brown the sugar in a pan, add the slivered almonds and toast lightly. Let cool. Melt the chocolate in a bowl placed in a pan of boiling water. Beat the egg whites with the lemon juice until they hold stiff peaks. Mix the beaten egg whites into the melted chocolate until you have obtained a smooth mixture. Whip the heavy cream until it holds stiff peaks, and fold loosely into the chocolate mixture together with the toasted, slivered almonds. Cover and put in a very cold place. This is a delicious dessert that is easy to prepare. For a different taste, try using the very finely chopped rind of an untreated orange instead of the slivered almonds.

Roast Apples

Whichever of the following four varieties you decide to make, roast apples will always be a pleasant and welcome dessert. In old times, housewives in the countryside simply put the apples in the oven or in the central hole of a tile stove and let them cook until they were tender and their skins were about to burst. Since then, many other delicious varieties have evolved.

No. 1

6-8 apples, of uniform size
4 Tbs raisins
4 Tbs rum
6 Tbs walnut meat, chopped
3 Tbs brown sugar
1-1 1/2 cups white wine
1 oz. butter

Wash the apples. With an apple corer, carefully pierce and cut out the stem, crown and core of each apple. Place the unpeeled apples in a fireproof dish. Prepare the following filling: Sprinkle the raisins with the rum, add the coarsely chopped walnuts and the sugar, mix well. Fill the apples with the raisin mixture. Add the wine to the apples in the dish, dot the apples with butter flakes, cover with aluminum foil and roast the apples in a 420°F oven for approx. 1/2 hour (depending on the kind of apple used).

No. 2

2 oz. marzipan, prepared
1 oz. confectioner's sugar
1 Tbs Arrack
2 Tbs candied ginger, chopped
2 Tbs almond flakes

Knead the marzipan with sugar and Arrack, until it crumbles, add the coarsely chopped ginger, mix, and fill the apples with the mixture. Sprinkle the apples with the almond flakes and proceed as directed in basic recipe above. A very good dessert !

No. 3

8 apples,
uniform size
5 Tbs hazelnuts,
toasted and ground
4 Tbs slivered almonds
2 Tbs raisins
3 egg whites
1/2 Tbs lemon juice
3 oz. sugar
2 Tbs almond flakes

Peel the apples and remove the cores, using an apple corer. Arrange the apples in a heatproof dish. Mix the hazelnuts, almonds, and raisins, fill the apples with the mixture, cover, and bake in a preheated 420-450°F oven for 15 minutes. Meanwhile, beat the egg whites with the lemon juice until they hold stiff peaks. Add the sugar and continue to beat until glossy. Decorate the cooked apples with batches of the egg white mixture, forming peaks. Sprinkle with almond flakes and brown briefly under the grill or with the oven set for top heat.

No. 4

8 Tbs cranberry
preserve
1 orange, untreated

Mix the cranberry preserve with the grated orange peel and fill the apples with the mixture. Proceed as directed in basic recipe on p. 132.

Stewed Rhubarb

2 lbs rhubarb
lemon juice
3 oz. sugar

Peel the rhubarbs thinly, working from the leaves down. Wash the rhubarbs, halve the stalks lengthwise and cut them crosswise into 2 in. pieces. Dribble lemon juice over the rhubarb pieces and sprinkle the sugar over them. Let the fruit draw for 1 hour. Simmer the fruit in its own juice, covered, over low heat. Serve cool. The lemon juice tones down the harsh taste of the rhubarb.

Apple Sauce

In earlier times apples which had fallen from the trees and were too small to peel, were used to make this dish. The apple sauce was particularly light when made with the first apples of the season, the so-called "clear apples." Any type of apple may be used, however. In most cases the addition of sugar will not be necessary.

3 lbs apples
1/2 lemon
 (untreated)

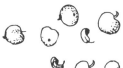

Wash the apples thoroughly and remove stems and crowns only. Quarter the apples but do not remove the cores, as they give the dish its delicious taste. Put the quartered apples and the lemon in a saucepan and add approx. 1 in. water. Bring to a boil and simmer over moderate heat until the apples are soft. Pass the apples through a sieve. Season and sweeten to taste. Apple sauce should never be served ice cold.

Apple Snow

2 egg whites

Beat the egg whites until they hold stiff peaks. Fold into boiling hot apple sauce (see above).

Bilberry Cup

1 lb - 1 1/2 lbs
 bilberries,
 fresh or frozen
3 Tbs sugar
1 cup red wine

1 cup heavy cream
1 Tbs vanilla
 sugar

In a heatproof bowl, sprinkle the bilberries with the sugar. Heat the red wine, add it to the bilberries and let them draw well. In a bowl, whip the heavy cream until it holds stiff peaks, and add the vanilla sugar. Arrange the berries with the red wine in individual serving glasses, and decorate with dabs of whipped cream. The red wine will bind the tannic acid of the bilberries. This is a delicious and quick dessert!

Stewed Plums

From Höchberg

Franconian plums are best for this recipe.

2 cups water
1/2 lemon, untreated, sliced
1/2 cinnamon stick
1/4 lb sugar
1 1/2 lbs plums

In a large saucepan, bring the water, lemon slices, cinnamon stick and sugar to a vigorous boil until the sugar is dissolved. Meanwhile, using a slotted ladle, dip the plums in batches into boiling water. Remove the skins but leave the plums whole. Take the lemon slices and cinnamon stick from the sugar and water mixture and add the plums. Simmer slowly, testing for texture. Do not overcook: Let the stewed plums cool, covered. -- Leaving the stones in will give the plums a pleasant, light taste of almonds.

Passau Elderberry Sauce

1 lb elderberries
1/2 lb pears
1/2 lb plums
1 cup water
4 Tbs sugar, or honey to taste
1 thick lemon slice (untreated)
1 in. cinnamon stick

Pick over the elderberries and remove all stems. Wash the berries. Drain them in a colander. Peel the pears, remove the cores and cut the pears into slivers. Wash and stone the plums. Add pears and plums to berries. In a large saucepan, bring the water to a boil, together with the sugar or honey, the lemon slice and the cinnamon, until the sugar is dissolved. Remove the spices and add the fruit to the boiling water. Simmer over low heat until done.

Zwetschgenpavesen

Recipe from grandma B. Fries.

Dried plums only may be used in the preparation of genuine Old Bavarian plum fritters.

1 lb dried plums
some water
1/2 cinnamon stick
1/2 lemon peel,
untreated
3 lumps sugar
6 white buns,
1-2 days old
some cold milk
4 eggs
clarified butter
sugar and cinnamon

Remove the stones from the plums, and chop the plums finely or put them through the meat grinder. Add a little water, the cinnamon, lemon peel and sugar lumps and cook until you have a thick pulp. Remove the spices.

Using a grater, remove the crusts from the buns. Cut the buns into 1/5 in. slices and fit them together in pairs. Fill each pair with a layer of plum pulp. Quickly dip the plum-filled "sandwiches" into cold milk on both sides, and stack to draw. Beat the eggs thoroughly with a fork, dip the fritters into the egg on both sides and fry, almost swimming, in hot clarified butter. Sprinkle with sugar and cinnamon, serve hot or cold.

from Lorle Schmidt Steinebach.

Topfennockerl

Upper Bavarian recipe

1 lb cottage cheese
4 eggs
large pinch salt
1-2 Tbs flour

Pass the cheese through a sieve, add the eggs and salt and mix until smooth. Blend in the flour (less flour is needed if the cheese is dry, more if it is very moist). In a large pot, bring lightly salted water to a boil. Using 2 teaspoons, drop small oval dumplings into the simmering water and let draw 5-8 minutes. With a slotted spoon, transfer the "Nockerln" to a colander to drain.

1 1/2 oz. butter
1 1/2 oz. sugar

Brown the butter and sugar in a pan. Add the Nockerln and coat them carefully with the butter-sugar mixture. Serve hot. Delicious!

Elder Blossom "Kücheln"

12-14 elder
blossoms
beer or wine batter
(p.141)
oil or clarified
butter, for frying
confectioner's sugar

Rinse blossoms, preferably in mineral water. Drain on paper towels. Dip them in beer or wine batter, shake off excess batter and fry the Kücheln in hot oil or clarified butter until crunchy and golden brown. Sprinkle generously with confectioner's sugar and serve hot.

Snow Balls in Vanilla Sauce

4 egg whites, very cold
4 cups milk
1 vanilla bean,
cut into bits
pinch of salt
1 tsp lemon juice
4 oz. sugar

In a wide saucepan, bring the milk to a boil with the vanilla bits. Beat the egg whites, with the salt and lemon juice, until they hold stiff peaks. Gradually add the sugar and continue to beat until stiff. Using two teaspoons, carefully shape oblong "Nockerln" and place them into the slowly simmering milk. Cook the "Nockerln" 4 minutes on one side, turn them carefully and cook another 4 min. on the other side. Lift the snowballs carefully from the milk and drain them on a sieve. Strain the milk.

1/2 cup sweet cream
4 egg yolks
2 Tbs vanilla sugar
2 Tbs sugar
1 Tbs cornstarch

Beat all ingredients together, add them to the hot milk and bring to a boil. Transfer the thickened liquid to a heat-proof glass dish, place the drained snowballs on top and brown them lightly under a grill or on the top rack of a very hot oven. (In old times this browning was done with a red-hot baking shovel!) Let cool, refrigerate, and serve cold. This dish is a particular favorite of children.

Drunken Maidens Red or White

3 eggs
3 Tbs hot water
1/2 lemon,untreated
5 oz. flour
fat for frying
freshly pressed
grape juice, red or
white wine sauce

Mix the eggs with the hot water and the grated lemon rind,stirring vigorously, until very foamy. Add the sifted flour and mix well.Using a tablespoon,cut oblong rolls from the dough and bake them in hot shortening to a golden brown color. Serve doused with hot, sweetened grape juice,or red or white wine sauce (p. 125).

Recipe
from
Aunt Nini

Nuns Buns

1 cup milk
pinch of salt
2 oz. butter
1 Tbs sugar
1/4 lb flour
3 eggs
fat for frying

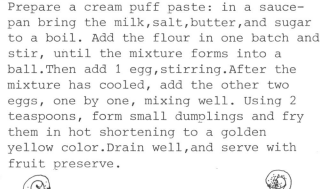

Prepare a cream puff paste: in a saucepan bring the milk,salt,butter,and sugar to a boil. Add the flour in one batch and stir, until the mixture forms into a ball.Then add 1 egg,stirring.After the mixture has cooled, add the other two eggs, one by one, mixing well. Using 2 teaspoons, form small dumplings and fry them in hot shortening to a golden yellow color.Drain well,and serve with fruit preserve.

Poor Knights

from Grossholzleute, Allgäu

These poor knights are not that poor at all! Cut a braided yeast bread "Hefezopf"(p.152), into 1/5 in. slices, soak them briefly in milk, coat them with beer dough "Bierteig" (p. 141), and fry them in hot shortening to a nice golden yellow color. Serve either with apple sauce (p. 134), or with vanilla sauce (p.125).

Very " Poor Knights " are made with bun slices.

Wine Chaudeau Cake   from Landshut

6 whole eggs
2 Tbs vanilla sugar
5 1/2 oz. sugar
* 3 1/2 oz. semi-sweet
baking chocolate,
grated
* 6 oz. hazelnuts,
lightly toasted
and ground
1 Tbs dark rum

In a heatproof bowl placed over a pot of
boiling water, beat the eggs with the
vanilla sugar and sugar until the mixture
is foamy, thick, and light in color.
Lightly fold chocolate and hazelnuts
into the mixture, add the rum and
pour the mixture into a well-buttered
10-in. spring form. Bake in a preheated
380°F oven for 1/2 hour, let cool on a
rack, unmold and serve on a deep platter, doused with wine chaudeau.

Wine Chaudeau

2 whole eggs
2 egg yolks
pinch of salt
5 Tbs sugar
1 Tbs cornstarch
1/2 lemon, untreated
1/2 cup milk
1 cup dry white wine
2 stiffly beaten
egg whites

In a heatproof pot beat the eggs, the egg
yolks, salt, sugar and cornstarch until
foamy. Add the paper-thin lemon peel (not
grated), then add the milk, and beat over
low heat until the mixture thickens
somewhat. Gradually beat in the wine.
When the mixture has again become hot,
discard the lemon peel and mix the
beaten egg whites into the hot sauce.

Puff

8 egg yolks
7 oz. sugar
7 oz. flour
1 lemon, untreated
1 oz. ea. chopped,
candied lemon rind,
raisins,
sultanas, slivered
almonds
8 egg whites
slivered almonds

Beat together egg yolks and sugar
until very foamy. Add the flour, the
grated lemon rind, the candied lemon
rind, berries and almonds. Beat the egg
whites until they hold stiff peaks
and lightly fold into the egg
yolk mixture. Bake in a buttered
soufflé dish lined with slivered almonds, in a preheated 410°F oven, for
3/4 hour. Pour hot red wine sauce
(p.125) over the puff and serve
immediately.

from Silly

Tapioca Soufflé

4 cups milk
1/2 lb tapioca
5 1/2 oz. butter
2 oz. sugar
1 lemon,untreated
6 egg yolks
1 tsp lemon juice
6 egg whites
1 1/2 oz.butter

Bring the milk to a boil, add the tapioca in a thin, steady stream, and let it draw at low heat approx. 10 minutes until it becomes glassy. Meanwhile, mix the butter with the grated lemon rind and egg yolks until very foamy. Add the cooled tapioca mixture in batches, and mix well. Beat the egg whites with the lemon juice until they hold stiff peaks, and fold into the tapioca mixture. Fill into a well-buttered soufflé dish, wipe the rim, dot with butter flakes, and bake on the center rack of a preheated 420°F oven 4o-45 minutes. Serve with stewed fruit.

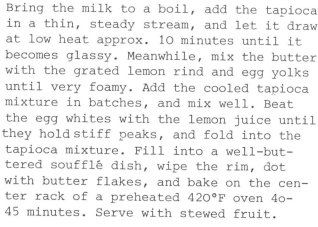

Nut Pudding

3 oz. butter
3 oz. sugar
1 Tbs vanilla sugar
3 egg yolks
6 oz. hazelnuts or
almonds,unpeeled
& finely grated
3 oz. semi-sweet
chocolate,grated
4 egg whites
1 tsp lemon juice

1 oz. butter
cake or cookie crumbs

1 1/2 cups heavy cream
sugar to taste
1 Tbs Kirsch

Mix the butter, sugar, vanilla sugar and egg yolks until foamy.Add the grated nuts and chocolate and mix well.Beat the egg whites with the lemon juice until they hold stiff peaks and fold them loosely into the nut mixture. Thickly butter a covered pudding form and coat with cake or cookie crumbs. Fill in the mixture,to reach approx. 1 1/2 in. from the rim. Fasten the cover, set the form in a pot of boiling water and bake at 420° F for a good hour. Remove from oven and let stand 5 minutes, then remove cover, let the steam subside and unmold the pudding.Whip the heavy cream, add sugar to taste, mix with the Kirsch, and serve the hot pudding coated with the whipped cream.

Beer or Wine Dough

9 oz. flour
1 cup beer -or-
1 cup wine
4 egg yolks
2 Tbs vegetable oil
3 egg whites
1/2 tsp salt

Sift the flour into a large bowl. Add the beer or wine in a steady stream and beat well to integrate. Add the egg yolks and oil and mix slowly. Let stand for 1 hour. In a separate bowl, beat the egg whites with the salt until they hold stiff peaks. Fold the egg whites into the beer or wine mixture.

Apple Rings

6-7 medium apples (mealy)
3 Tbs granulated sugar
3 Tbs rum
1 Tbs lemon juice

Peel the apples and remove the cores with an apple corer. Cut the apples into 1/2 in. rings and place the rings in a bowl. Sprinkle with the sugar, pour the rum and lemon juice over the rings, and cover. Let stand until you prepare a beer dough (above).

clarified butter, oil, or other shortening (for frying)
sugar and cinnamon

In a wide, flat saucepan, or a deep frying pan (at least 2 in. deep) heat the shortening. Dip the apple rings into the dough and fry them, a few at a time, until golden brown. Do not let the shortening get too hot! Drain the fried apple rings on paper towels, sprinkle with sugar and cinnamon, and serve hot.

Rabbit Ears

4 1/2 oz. flour
pinch of salt
1 1/2 oz. butter
1 whole egg
1 egg yolk
1 Tbs thick cream

shortening
cinnamon sugar

Sift the flour onto a pastry board, add the salt and butter cut into small pieces, the egg, egg yolk and cream and knead quickly into a dough. Let rest for 1/2 hr. in a cool place. Roll out on the floured pastry board and cut into 3 in. squares with a knife or a serrated roller. Cut a slit in the middle of each square, pull one corner through the slit and fry the *rabbit ears* in hot, deep fat to a golden color. Sprinkle with cinnamon sugar and serve hot or cold, with a cup of coffee.

Aunt Rosa's "Gaggerlschmarrn"

3 eggs
1 Tbs flour
2 Tbs milk
pinch of salt
1 Tbs raisins
approx.
1 1/2 oz.butter
confectioner's
sugar

In a bowl, beat together the eggs,flour,milk and salt.Carefully add the raisins.In a frying pan, heat the butter (do not let it become too hot!). Add the egg mixture (it should be about 1 in. high), and let it set at low heat until the underside is a golden yellow.Carefully turn it over and fry on the other side.Using a baking spatula,cut the pancake into cubes approx.1 in. square. Sprinkle with confectioner's sugar and serve with fruit preserve.

Pancakes

1/2 lb flour
pinch of salt
1/2 cup milk
1 cup mineral
water or club
soda
4 eggs
butter & oil
jam
cottage cheese
filling
confectioner's
sugar

In a bowl,mix the flour,salt,milk and mineral water until smooth.Add the eggs,beat briefly with a wire whisk, and let stand 1 hour. -- In a long-handled frying pan,heat up enough butter and oil to cover the bottom of the pan. Coat the pan with the pancake batter,tilting the pan for even distribution. Bake to a golden color on both sides.Serve hot,filled with jam or a cottage cheese filling, or with stewed fruit on the side, and sprinkled with confectioner's sugar.

Strudel Dough Basic recipe

1/2 lb flour
2 eggs
pinch of salt
2 Tbs oil
1/2 cup water

Sift the flour onto a pastry board and make a well in the center. Break the eggs into the well,add the salt,oil and water,and mix all with the flour,working outwards from the center.Then knead the dough until it becomes smooth and silky.Let it rest for 1/2 hour,covered with a warm saucepan.Then roll out on a floured cloth and "pull out" to the desired thickness (very thin), with the backs of your hands.

Cottage Cheese "Strudel"

Serves 6-8 persons as dessert   4-5 persons as main dish.

Prepare " Strudel" dough, following the basic recipe, p.142.

3 lbs cherries, washed and stoned
3 lbs cottage cheese (dry)

4 egg yolks
2 1/2 oz. sugar
1 lemon (untreated)
4 cold egg whites

Pass the cheese through a sieve. Mix with the egg yolks, sugar, and grated lemon rind. Beat the egg whites with 1 tsp lemon juice, until they hold stiff peaks. Fold loosely into the cheese mixture.

2 oz. butter
ground cinnamon,
   to taste

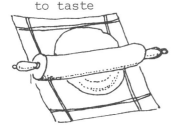

melted butter

2 cups milk,
   boiling hot
confectioner's
   sugar

Brush the pulled-out Strudel dough with the warm, melted butter. Distribute half the cheese mixture evenly over the dough and dot with half of the cherries. Sprinkle with cinnamon. Fold in the edges of the dough and, with the help of the table-cloth, roll up the Strudel very loosely (the cheese mixture expands while baking!) Slide the Strudel into a well-buttered baking pan or fireproof dish. Proceed in the same way with the second Strudel. Brush both Strudels with melted butter. Bake in pre-heated 450°F oven 35-45 minutes, brushing the Strudels with melted butter a few more times while baking. Just before end of baking time, pour the hot milk over the Strudels and let them draw to the end of baking time. Sprinkle with sugar.

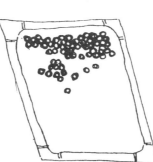

Munich Apple "Strudel"

In contrast to the famous Apple Strudel of Vienna which is baked on a baking sheet, its Munich relative is a juicy affair and is prepared in a baking pan or fireproof dish. Apple Strudel may be stored in a freezer. It is therefore recommended to make double or triple quantities at one time and freeze some of it for later use.

Prepare Strudel dough, following instructions in basic recipe, p. 142 . (Allow 2 Strudels as dessert for 4-6 persons, or as a main dish for 3-4 persons.)

3 lbs tart apples
juice of 1 lemon
5 oz. raisins)
5 Tbs rum) soak
3 oz. butter
1 cup thick sour
 cream
sugar)
cinnamon) to taste

Peel, core and quarter the apples. Using a vegetabele slicer, cut them into thin slices;sprinkle with lemon juice to avoid discoloration. Brush the pulled-out Strudel dough with the warm melted butter, dab the sour cream over the butter and distribute it evenly. Spread the apple slices over the dough in an even layer, stopping short about 1 in. from the edge of the dough. Sprinkle with the rum-soaked raisins, sugar and cinnamon. Fold in the edges of the dough and, with the help of the tablecloth, roll up the Strudel loosely. Slide the Strudel into the well-buttered baking pan. Proceed in the same manner with the second Strudel. Pre-heat oven to 470°F.

1 cup milk
1 cup heavy cream

Confectioner's
 sugar

Bring milk and cream to a boil, and pour over the Strudels in the pan. Bake on middle rack of oven for 45-60 minutes, diminishing oven heat to 420°F. Cut into portions before serving and sprinkle with sifted sugar. Serve hot or cold.

Bread Torte

3 oz. stale dark bread
Schwarzbrot, grated
4 Tbs hot red wine
10 egg yolks
7 oz. sugar
8 1/2 oz. almonds,
unpeeled, grated
2 oz. candied lemon
rind, finely chopped
1 Tbs cinnamon, ground
1/2 tsp cloves, ground
1/2 tsp cardamom, ground
10 egg whites

Douse the dark breadcrumbs with the hot
red wine and soak. Mix the egg yolks
with the sugar, stirring vigorously until the mixture has a white foam, then
add the almonds, candied lemon rind, and
soaked breadcrumbs.

Add the spices to the mixture. Beat the
egg whites until they hold stiff peaks,
and lightly fold them into mixture.
Preheat oven to 360° F. In a well-buttered 10 in. springform coated with
breadcrumbs, bake the mixture for 1 hour.
Unmold the cake on a rack. When it has
cooled completely, (preferably the
following day) cut the cake into two

5 Tbs dark rum
- mixed with -
10 Tbs red wine
3 oz. apricot jam

halves and sprinkle both layers with
rum and wine mixture. Spread one half
with apricot jam and top with the other
half in such a way that the bottom of
the cake, as you baked it, is now on top.
Spread the top thinly with jam passed
through a sieve, and let dry briefly.

5 oz. raw marzipan
1 1/2 oz. confectioner's
sugar
6 oz. chocolate glaze
or 6 oz. semi-sweet
chocolate

Knead together the marzipan and sugar,
roll out to a round layer and cover
the cake with it.
Melt the ready-made chocolate glaze or
the semi-sweet chocolate in a bowl
placed into boiling water, stir until
smooth, then cover the cake (top and
sides) with it. Decorate attractively

candied fruit

with candied fruits.

Sponge Cake

Here is an old family recipe, for a 10 in. dia. spring form.

e/w = egg weight (see recipe for Fruit Cake p. 149).

5 e/w flour
6 e/w sugar
6 whole eggs
1 Tbs rum
vanilla sugar
lemon rind
(untreated)

In a heatproof bowl placed atop a pot of boiling water, beat the sugar with the eggs until white and foamy, but do not allow it to become more then lukewarm. Take the bowl from the heat and blend in the rum. Add vanilla sugar or grated lemon rind, to taste. Loosely fold in the flour. In a thickly buttered spring form coated with stale white breadcrumbs, bake the cake in a pre-heated 380°F oven approx. 3/4 hour, testing with a wooden stick (toothpick) whether the cake is done. Let the cake cool on a rack.

Sponge cake may be used in many different ways.-- For example:

1. For a quick, festive cake, cut the sponge cake into 3 layers and fill with 1/2 lb sliced fruit and 2 cups sweetened whipped cream.

2. For a tea cake: add 1 oz. ea. raisins, peeled slivered almonds, candied lemon rind and candied orange rind (both finely diced) to the batter and bake in a deep oblong cake pan.

3. For Easter, bake in lamb-shaped molds.

4. For an aniseed cake, blend 1 1/2 Tbs ground aniseed into the batter.

No limits are set to your imagination.

Prinzregententorte

This "Torte" was created for Prince Regent Luitpold, its 8 layers symbolizing the 8 governmental districts, i.e.: Upper Bavaria, Lower Bavaria, Upper Palatinate, Upper Franconia, Central Franconia, Lower Franconia, Swabia, and the left-bank Rhine Palatinate which belonged to Bavaria in the years 1815-1946. It remains open to debate, however, which Bavarian district lies on the chocolate side ...

1/2 lb sweet cream butter	Stir the butter vigorously until foamy.
1/2 lb sugar pinch of salt 1 Tbs vanilla sugar 1 Tbs dark rum 2 whole eggs 2 egg yolks	Gradually add alternating small portions of the marked ingredients, and beat all until you have a loose, foamy mixture.
1/2 lb flour 2 egg whites, beaten with 1/2 tsp lemon juice	Add the sifted flour, mix, then carefully fold the stiffly beaten egg whites. Spread the bottom of a well-buttered springform (without the spring ring) with approx. 2 Tbs of the mixture, making it thicker around the edge so it does not brown too fast. Bake 8 layers this way, using the middle rack of

a preheated 350°F oven. Baking time is 6-8 minutes each. Cool the layers on an even surface, then layer them with greaseproof paper in a stack and weight with a heavy object to make them flat. Prepare the following filling:

7 oz. semi-sweet chocolate 7 oz. butter 4 oz. sugar 3 egg yolks	Melt the chocolate in a bowl placed into boiling water. In a large bowl, stir the butter and sugar vigorously until very foamy, add the egg yolks and the cooled chocolate. Spread the filling evenly on the individual

cake layers and put the layers on top of each other on a serving plate. The top layer should be left free: gently brush off any crumbs, spread it with a thin layer of apricot jam, let it dry briefly, then coat it with smooth chocolate glaze, using the ready-made type by heating it up, mixing it well, and spreading it hot over the Torte. Smooth the glaze with a knife on top and sides. Let the cake stand for 1 day before serving. This cake is a real treat!

Fruit Cake "Egg Weight"

(may be made with cherries, apricots, peaches, plums, apples)

This cake will always be perfect because the size of the eggs determines the exact weight of the other ingredients. The eggs are weighed, and their weight is to be taken as a measure. (NOTE: "e/w" in the list of ingredients indicates "egg weight".)

2 e/w butter
3 e/w sugar
3 whole eggs
1 lemon (untreated)
2 e/w flour
2 Tbs rum
stale breadcrumbs,
    as needed
1 lb cherries, washed

Mix the butter and sugar until foamy. Add the eggs, one at a time, and the grated lemon rind. Gradually add the sifted flour. Pour into a well-buttered spring form lined with breadcrumbs. Add the cherries, distributed evenly over the batter. Do not remove the cherry stones (they taste better with the stones left inside)!

For Apple Cake:

* 1-1 1/2 lb smallish
    apples

* 3 Tbs hazelnuts,
    ground
2 Tbs sugar
1 tsp cinnamon,ground

Peel, halve or quarter, and core the apples. Cut them into "fans" (achieved by not cutting all the way through the apple halves or quarters, and spreading them into a tight fan shape).
Distribute the apples over the batter. Sprinkle the dish with the hazelnuts, sugar and cinnamon, and bake approx. 45 minutes in a 420° F oven. The fruit will sink into the batter while baking.

For Peach Cake/Apricot Cake:

* 1-1 1/2 lbs peaches
    or apricots
* 3 Tbs almonds,
    slivered

Scald the peaches briefly with boiling water, skin and halve them and place them over the batter. Sprinkle with the almonds. Proceed in the same way for Apricot Cake.

For Plum Cake:

* 1 lb plums, washed,
    stoned and halved

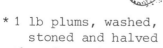

Place the prepared plums over the batter.

When done, invert the cake immediately onto a cake rack. After cooling, reverse it onto a platter. Sprinkle with sugar before serving. Delicious if served with a bowl of whipped cream!

Apple Cake

10 oz. flour	Sift the flour onto a
1/4 lb butter	pastry board. Add the
1/4 lb sugar	butter, in flakes,
2 whole eggs	sprinkle with the sugar and add the eggs and
1 Tbs rum	rum. Mix and knead quickly to a dough, and
2 lbs apples	let rest for 1/2 hour, covered. Peel and
1 oz. butter	thinly slice the apples (use a tart, mealy
* 4 Tbs raisins	sort), sauté them briefly in the butter (3-4
(soaked in rum)	mins.) and let them cool. Roll out smaller
* 2 Tbs candied	half of dough into a circle large enough to
orange peel,	cover bottom and sides of a ·1o-in. buttered
chopped	spring form. Mix apple slices, raisins and

orange peel and fill into the lined form.
Roll out remaining dough to cover top of cake;
press edges to seal. Punch holes into top
layer to allow steam to escape.

1 egg yolk	Brush top with egg yolk and garnish with
* 2 Tbs almonds	almond halves, pressing down firmly to hold.
	Bake in preheated 420° F oven 40 - 45 minutes.
3 1/2 oz. con-	Mix the sifted sugar with the liquids and pour
fectioner's sugar	over the hot cake. Let cool before removing
1 Tbs Arrack	spring form. Serve with a bowl of whipped cream.
1 Tbs hot water	

Rhubarb Cake

2 lbs rhubarbs	Cut the thinly peeled rhubarbs in 2-in. bits,
3 1/2 oz.sugar	mix with the sugar and braise at low heat
	until done but still firm. Prepare a short-
shortcake dough	cake dough following the basic recipe above,
	roll it out to fit a large (11-12 in.) but-
7 egg whites	tered spring form, and bake it 25 minutes at
1 Tbs. lemon juice	450° F. Arrange the drained rhubarb on top.
7 oz.sugar	Beat egg whites and lemon juice until stiff,
	gradually beat in the sugar, heap the mixture
3 Tbs almond	onto the cake and make a pattern of peaks
flakes	with the help of a fork. Sprinkle with almond
	flakes and brown briefly under top heat.

Bilberry Cake

Prepare a yeast dough following the basic recipe on p. 123, and using the following ingredients:
3/4 lb flour, 3/4 oz. yeast, 1 cup milk, 3 oz. sugar, pinch of salt, 1 egg, 1/8 lb butter, 1 Tbs lard.
Place the rolled-out dough onto a small, buttered baking sheet; the dough should have on overhang so it can be folded over the filling:

1 oz. melted butter
*2 lbs bilberries
sugar and
cinnamon, ground

Brush the dough with the melted butter, and arrange the washed and very well drained bilberries on top. Fold the overhanging edges over the sides. On the middle rack of a preheated 420° F oven, bake the cake 25-30 minutes. Remove from the oven and sprinkle the hot cake with sugar and cinnamon, to taste. This cake tastes best when served fresh. It will also keep well in the freezer.

Plum Squares

Prepare a yeast dough following the basic recipe on p. 123, and using the following ingredients:
3/4 lb flour, 3/4 oz. yeast, 1/2 cup milk, 1 egg, 1/8 lb butter, 1 Tbs lard, 3 oz. sugar, pinch of salt.

3 lbs plums
sugar and
cinnamon, ground

While the dough is rising, wash, drain, and stone the plums, then cut the halves lengthwise along the middle again, but not quite through (see sketch) to make them lie flat; or use a stone-remover gadget, which will do all this in one operation. Spread the risen and rolled-out dough onto a buttered baking sheet, and arrange the plums in a roof-tile pattern on top. Connoisseurs maintain that the plums should "stand" rather than lay
flat, i.e., they should be tightly packed. On the middle rack of a preheated 420°F oven, bake the cake 25-30 minutes. Remove from the oven, sprinkle the hot cake with sugar and cinnamon, to taste, and cut in squares when cooled.

Pleated Yeast Bread

Prepare yeast dough, following the basic recipe on p.123, and let it rise.

1/4 lb raisins
1/4 lb candied lemon rind, chopped
1/4 lb candied orange rind, chopped

1 egg
3 Tbs coarse sugar
* 3 Tbs slivered almonds

Dust the raisins with flour, and mix them, together with the lemon and orange rind, both chopped very small, into the dough. Separate the dough into 3 even parts, form the parts into thick rolls and pleat them to a loaf. Place the loaf onto a buttered and floured baking sheet, pinching the ends together and folding them neatly under. Let the loaf rise briefly (approx. 10 minutes) once more. Beat the egg slightly and pour over the hollows in the dough. Sprinkle with sugar and almonds. Bake 50-60 minutes in a pre-heated 390°F oven. Tastes best when fresh. May be deep-frozen.

Cheesecake

Prepare a shortcake dough using 1 1/2 times the amount described in the recipe for Applecake, p. 150 , or a yeast dough, using 1/2 times the amount described in the basic Yeast Dough recipe, p. 123 .

2 lbs cottage cheese ("Topfen" or dry "Quark," p. 168)
1 cup sour cream
6 eggs
1/4 lb sugar
2 Tbs flour
2 oz. butter
2 oz. raisins
1 lemon, untreated
2 egg yolks
4 Tbs sweet cream
confectioner's sugar

Pass the cottage cheese through a sieve, gradually add the sour cream, eggs, sugar, and flour, and mix well. Warm the butter and add to the mixture, together with the raisins and the grated lemon rind. Roll out the shortcake or yeast dough and fit it onto a buttered baking sheet. Spread the cheese mixture over the dough evenly. Preheat the oven to 420°F. Beat the egg yolks with the sweet cream until well mixed and brush the top of the cheese mixture with the egg wash. Bake the cake on the middle rack of the oven for approx. 1/2 hour. Sprinkle with confectioner's sugar and cut up the cake into 3 in. squares. The cake - called "Käsblotz" in Franconia - tastes best when lukewarm.

Easter Bread

1 lemon, untreated
1 lemon, untreated
2 oz. sultanas

Prepare a yeast dough, following the recipe on p.123 , and adding the grated rind of one lemon and the washed and well-drained sultanas. After the dough has risen, shape it into two loaves, place the loaves on a buttered and floured baking sheet and let them rise once more.

Brush the loaves with egg yolk. Using a sharp knife or razor blade, trace a deep diamond pattern into the tops and bake in a preheated 390°F oven approx. 1 hour, until golden yellow. Let the loaves cool on a rack. Easter bread will stay fresh for a few days if wrapped in aluminium foil.-- The tradidional

Easter Breakfast

slices of Easter Bread are spread with butter and garnished with cooked ham and paper-thin slices of horseradish.These are served with hard-boiled eggs,dyed or painted in the traditional manner, hidden by the Easter Bunny and subsequently found by the children. Easter Breakfast in Bavaria always includes an apple,in memory of Adam and Eve. A small, separate basket containing a bit of everything is taken to Church to be blessed by the first person to get up.

"Kücheln"

Fried Bavarian Doughnuts

These doughnuts are a must at every church fair and Heaven help the cook who does not have a sufficient quantity on hand!

Prepare yeast dough, following the basic recipe on p.123 but using 1 cup - 1 1/2 cups milk rather then the 1/2 cup specified, to achieve a soft consistency. After beating the dough to its required smoothness, do not let it rise. With the help of a tablespoon, cut dumplings from the dough and place them on a pastry board. Brush them with oil or melted butter. Let them rest briefly, so they expand only slightly. Then "pull" them outward, beginning from the inside, so that a ring forms, held together by only a paper-thin layer of dough. Fry the doughnuts swimming in clarified butter, turning them once very carefully to ensure that no shortening gets into the "window," which must remain very light in color. Serve the hot/warm doughnuts sprinkled with confectioner's sugar.

Church Fair Doughnuts

Prepare a yeast dough following the basic recipe on p.123 but using 1 cup milk and 1/2 cup thick cream. After the dough has risen, form dumplings as described in the recipe for Yeast Dumplings ("Rohrnudeln"), p.126 . Let them rise briefly. Using scissors,cut a cross in the top of each dumpling. Fry them loosely swimming in clarified butter until golden yellow. Do not overheat the frying fat! They are done in approx. 10 min., and should be served well drained and cooled and sprinkled with confectioner's sugar.

Carnival Doughnuts

Prepare a yeast dough following the basic recipe (p.123) but with 1-1 1/2 cups milk to make the dough soft and pliable. After the dough has risen, roll it out to a large quadrangle 1/2 in. thick. Lightly mark half of the dough with a 3 in. cookie cutter or a wine glass, keeping the circles close to each other.Do not press all the way through the dough!Put 1/2 tsp firm jam(e.g.,apricot, rose hip, raspberry and red currant, mixed) into the center of each circle. Fold the other half of the dough over the first half. Using the same cookie cutter or wine glass, press down firmly and cut out the doughnuts. Place the doughnuts, well apart, on a lightly floured board, cover with a cloth, and let them rise to approx. double height. Dust off superfluous flour.In

clarified butter or oil

confectioner's sugar

fry the doughnuts,putting them into the shortening top down first.Cover the pan with a folded cloth.When one side of the doughnuts has browned, turn them around and fry them on the other side.This is the time when they are supposed to rise and develop a light-colored "midriff". Cooking time is approx. 7-8 minutes altogether. - Drain the doughnuts on paper towels; sprinkle with confectioner's sugar. Carnival Doughnuts are served not only at Carnival time,but also on New Year's Eve with punch.

Cream Puffs "Eclairs"

1/2 cup water
2 1/2 oz. butter
pinch of salt
4 1/2 oz. flour
4 eggs

Bring the water to a boil with the butter and salt. Add all the flour at the same time, and stir until the mixture separates from the sides of the pan and forms a ball. Take from the stove and mix in one whole egg. Let the mixture cool. After cooling, mix in the remaining 3 eggs, one at a time. Butter and flour a baking sheet. With two teaspoons, or using a pastry bag, form small heaps of the dough on the baking sheet. Bake 30 minutes in a pre-heated 420°F oven. Turn off the oven, do not open oven door, and let the puffs cool inside the oven for 20 minutes. Then take the baking sheet from the oven, place it on a cake rack, let the puffs cool completely and cut small caps from the top of the puffs.

1 1/2 cups heavy cream
1 Tbs vanilla sugar

Filling: Whip the cream until it holds stiff peaks. Mix the vanilla sugar into the whipped cream, and fill the puffs with the mixture. Replace the caps, and sprinkle with confectioner's sugar.

"Strauben"

Prepare a cream-puff paste (above). Cut grease-proof paper into 6-in. squares (approx. 10 squares). Heat some oil or shortening in a pan, dip the paper squares into the frying fat and place them on a tray lined with aluminium foil. Using a pastry bag fitted with a large-holed decorator tip, spiral rings onto the paper squares. Let the rings glide from the squares into the frying fat. Bake 4 minutes on each side, drain on paper towels, sprinkle with confectioner's sugar, and serve with coffee. They are delicious!

Christmas Loaf

Prepare a yeast dough following the basic recipe (p. 123), but using 6 oz. butter. After beating the dough, add:
2 1/2 oz. ea. sultanas, raisins, candied orange rind (diced), candied lemon rind (diced), slivered almonds. ***

After the dough has risen (you may stretch out this process over-night by keeping the dough in a cool room), form an oblong loaf on a pastry board; with a rolling pin, flatten the middle part and fold one side of the dough over the flat part to obtain the typical Stollen shape. Smooth the surface with your hand and push under the dough any ingredients that may be sticking out as they will become hard and dark during baking. Dust a baking sheet with flour (do not butter it as that will cause the Stollen to "run" sideways). Brush the Stollen with melted butter and let stand while you preheat the oven to 410°F. Bake 1 1/4 hours, testing with a wooden stick. Cool the Stollen on a rack, spread butter on it, and sift a thick layer of confectioner's sugar over it. A Stollen should be allowed to rest for a few days before serving. It may also be frozen and can thus be prepared before the general Christmas baking time.

 Fruit Loaf

Soak 1/4 lb ea. dried pear slices, plums and apricot halves in lukewarm water 3 hours; drain and dice the fruit. Finely dice 2 1/2 oz. ea. nuts, figs and candied lemon rind, sprinkle with 2 Tbs Arrack, add to the fruit together with 5 oz. sugar, and spice with 2 Tbs ground cinnamon, 1 tsp ground cloves,and 1 tsp ground cardamom. Of 1 1/2 lb rye bread dough obtained from the baker's, mix 1 lb with the above ingredients and shape two loaves. Halve the remaining dough, roll out two leaves, and roll each loaf into a "cover". Let rise 3/4 hour in a warm place. Brush with a mixture of honey and water and bake 1 hour at 400°F. Tastes best after a rest of 3 days, with butter spread on the slices.

Christstollen

Kletzenbrot

Ansbach Cookies

1/2 lb flour
2 oz. sugar
1 Tbs vanilla sugar
5 oz. butter

Sift the flour onto a pastry board, sprinkle with the sugar and vanilla sugar, and dot with the butter cut into flakes. Knead it all rapidly to a dough and put in a cool place to rest for 1 hour. Sprinkle the pastry board with flour, roll out the dough approx. 1/8 in. thick and cut into various shapes with cookie cutters. Put in a cool place again briefly. On the middle rack of a 400° F oven, bake the cookies approx. 8 minutes. Optional: brush the cookies with beaten egg yolk and garnish with almond flakes.

Aniseed Loaves

2 whole eggs
6 1/2 oz. sugar
1 Tbs vanilla sugar
6 1/2 oz. flour, sifted
1 Tbs aniseed, ground

Ansbach

All ingredients should be slightly warmed! Beat the eggs slightly in a fireproof dish. Add the sugar and vanilla sugar. Place the dish on top of a pot of boiling water. Beat the batter until it turns thick and frothy, but do not let it become more than lukewarm. Take the dish off the boiling water and loosely fold in the flour and aniseed. Using two teaspoons, form round cookies onto a buttered and floured baking sheet. There should be no peaks in the center of the cookies, or they will not rise! Using one of the spoons, roll in the edges of each cookie (see drawing). Let the cookies stand in a warm room overnight or, if possible, for a whole day, to dry. The surface of the cookies must be dull before they may be baked. Place an empty baking sheet on the top rack of the pre-heated 310°F oven, to act as a shield for the cookies which should remain white on top, while their "feet" should become light brown. Bake 12-15 minutes on the middle rack. Store in a metal cooky bin.

Hazelnut Cookies

1/4 lb flour
*1/4 lb hazelnuts,
lightly toasted
and ground
1/4 lb sugar
1 Tbs vanilla sugar
1/4 lb butter
chocolate glaze
hazelnuts, whole

Sift the flour onto a pastry board, add the hazelnuts, sugar, vanilla sugar and flaked butter, and knead rapidly to a dough. Shape the dough into a roll of approx. 1 1/2 in. dia., and put in a cool place. Cut 1 in. rounds from the roll and arrange them on a cookie sheet lined with baking foil. Refrigerate once more. In a preheated 350° F oven, bake the cookies approx. 10 minutes. Cover with chocolate glaze while still hot, and decorate each cookie with a whole hazelnut. Let the cookies cool at room temperature.

Nürnberg Spiced Cookies

4 Tbs honey
1 lb brown sugar
4 eggs
1 1/2 Tbs cinnamon,
ground
1/2 tsp cloves,
ground
1/2 tsp cardamom,
ground
* 2 1/2 oz. candied
lemon peel, and
* 2 oz. candied
orange peel,
finely chopped
* 2 1/2 oz. walnuts,
coarsely chopped
* 2 oz. almonds, ground
1 1/5 lbs flour
1 tsp baking soda

Warm up the honey in a saucepan, add the sugar and eggs, and beat the mixture until very foamy. Add the spices, fruit, and nuts. Sift together the flour and baking soda and add to the mixture. Mix well, then knead all into a dough. Cover, or put into a freezer bag, and let the dough rest for 1 day at room temperature. Next day, form small, cherry-sized balls and arrange them on a buttered and floured cooky sheet. Bake on the middle rack of a preheated 350°F oven approx. 15 minutes. These cookies have to be left standing a few days before serving, but they also keep fresh for a long time in a metal box (8 weeks).

Meringue Rings

4 egg whites
(at least 4
days old and
well cooled)
1 tsp lemon juice
8 oz. sugar

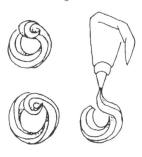

In a heatproof dish placed over a pot of boiling water, beat the egg whites with the lemon juice and sugar until they hold stiff peaks. Add food coloring, if desired. Spoon into a pastry bag fitted with a decorator tip and spiral into rings or any desired shape onto a buttered and floured baking sheet or a baking sheet lined with buttered and floured aluminum foil. Sprinkle with coarse sugar. Let stand briefly, to dry. Pre-heat oven to 300° F and dry the meringue rings slowly at low temperature, to prevent browning. After baking, let stand to cool before removing the rings from the baking sheet. Mix the rings with the Christmas cookies, or hang them from the Christmas tree with colored ribbons, or use them to decorate Christmas packages.

Rose Hip Baisers

3 egg whites
(3 1/2 oz.)
1 tsp lemon juice
7 oz. sugar
5 oz. rose hip
paste (raw)
*6 oz. almonds,
blanched,
and grated
1 1/2 in. baking
wafers
rose hip jam

In a heatproof dish placed over a pot of boiling water, beat the egg whites with the lemon juice and sugar until the mixture is firm enough to handle. Spoon 6 Tbs of the mixture into a pastry bag fitted with a decorator tip and put it into the refrigerator. Lightly fold the rose hip paste and the almonds into the mixture and immediately form and place small, round mounds of 1 in. dia. onto baking wafers set on a cooky sheet. With the handle of a wooden cooking spoon, make small wells into the top of each mound and fill these with rose hip jam. With the refrigerated decorator bag, form small dots on top of the jam-filled wells. Let stand for 1/2 hour, to dry. In an oven pre-heated to 300°F dry rather than bake the baisers 30-40 minutes. You should be able to crush the underside of these cookies, otherwise they become too hard. Place them into freezer bags for storage.

Elise's Gingerbread   from Nürnberg

3 eggs
1/2 lb sugar
1 Tbs vanilla sugar

*1/2 lb hazelnuts,
 lightly toasted
 and ground
*1/8 lb candied lemon
 rind,finely chopped
*1/2 lb candied orange
 rind,finely chopped
1/4 cup milk,lukewarm
1 Tbs flour
1 Tbs cinnamon,ground
1/2 tsp cloves,ground
1 lemon rind,grated

round wafers
approx. 2 in. dia
*almonds,peeled
 and halved
*candied lemon rind,
 sliced

7 oz.confectioner's
sugar
1-2 Tbs hot water
2 Tbs. Arrack

In a heatproof bowl placed over a pot
of boiling water, beat together the
eggs,sugar,and vanilla sugar until very
foamy. The mixture should get lukewarm
at the most!

Take the bowl from the heat and add all
the marked ingredients,mixing them in
loosly.

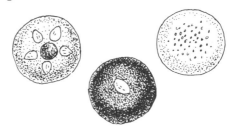

Spread the mixture on round wafers,keep-
ing it approx.1/2 in.thick in the middle
and sloping toward the sides. Decorate
in attractive patterns with almond
halves and candied lemon rind. Let the
rounds dry slightly before baking, then
bake them slowly (approx. 20 minutes)
in a preheated 270°F oven. It should be
possible to press in slightly the underside of the rounds,otherwise they will
be too dry. Glaze with the following
mixture while still hot:

mix the sifted sugar with the hot water
and Arrack. Optional: color with food
coloring. Spread on top of the hot gin-
gerbread rounds. Let the rounds dry,and
store them in a metal box. They are best
when fresh.-You might try covering them
with a chocolate glaze p.148.In that case,decorate after glazing.

"Jumpers" Springerle

Two regions in Bavaria claim this specialty: Swabia, where it is called "Springerle" (Jumpers) and Nürnberg, where its name is "Eierzucker" (Egg-and-Sugar). In both places "Jumpers" are prepared in the same way. Since they have to rest at least 14 days before serving, it is advisable to start baking early! The main requisite is a set of wooden molds into which the dough is pressed to obtain various shapes. All ingredients should be lukewarm.

4 eggs
1 lb sugar
1 Tbs vanilla sugar
1/2 tsp salt of hartshorn
dash of Kirsch
1 lb flour
cornstarch

Mix the eggs, sugar, and vanilla sugar until foamy; 1 hour by hand will make the cookies come out best, or use an electric mixer at low speed, beating until the mixture is almost white and thickly foamy. Dissolve the hartshorn in the Kirsch, and mix into the lukewarm, sifted flour, add the egg mixture and knead all into a firm dough. Pack the dough into a moist cloth and let rest 1 hour. Roll out small portions of the dough 1/5 in. thick, finely sift some cornstarch onto the rounds, smoothing them with the ball of your hand. Press a mold onto the dough, cut off the edges (or use a small cutting wheel), lay the molded cookies onto a buttered and floured baking sheet and let them dry 24 hours in a warm room. First bake a test "Jumper" in the center of a 370°F oven for 1/2 hour. The surface should remain white, and the "Jumpers" should have slightly yellow "feet". If the test "Jumper" does not expand while baking, wet the bottom of the others as this is an indication that the dough is too dry.

The cooled "Jumpers" may be painted with food coloring to hang on the Christmas tree or as decorations for presents. They will always give pleasure!

Quince Cheese

Quince Cheese is related in no way to cheese – but, strangely enough, in Spain a type of quince paste is eaten with cheese ! In the old Bavarian town of Altötting quince cheese (called *Kittenkäs*) is sold in small boxes made of wood shavings. In Old Bavaria, a plate of Christmas cookies is incomplete without chunks of quince cheese.

5 lbs quinces

granulated sugar (for quantity, see text)

Rub the wool off the fruit with a wet rag. Remove stems and crowns. Wash the fruit. In a pot, add water to the quinces to barely cover. Bring to a boil and simmer, covered, approx. 1 hour or until tender. Peel and core the hot fruit and purée it through a sieve or in a blender. Weigh the purée. To 1 lb purée, add 1 lb sugar and 5 Tbs of the cooking liquid. In a heavy saucepan or, better, in a copper pot, cook slowly at moderate heat, stirring constantly, until the mixture thickens exposing bottom of pot when stirred and falls in heavy lumps from the spoon. While still hot, fill into molds (preferably copper) rinsed with cold water, or spread in an approx. 1 in. layer on a glass or china board, to be cut into cubes later. Let dry thoroughly. Quince cheese will keep 1 year if stored in covered glass or china jars.

Mocha Pralines

2 oz. butter
1 egg yolk
1 Tbs vanilla sugar
3 1/2 oz. confectioner's sugar
2 Tbs cocoa powder
5 oz. Mocha-flavored semi-sweet chocolate
confectioner's sugar, chocolate coffee beans

In a bowl, mix the butter and egg yolk until fluffy. Add the sifted sugar, vanilla and cocoa, mixing well. Melt the chocolate in a bowl, let it cool and add it to the sugar mixture. Form oblong pralines with 2 teaspoons, place them on aluminum foil and refrigerate. Sprinkle with sugar and decorate with chocolate *coffee beans*. Store in cool place.

Miscellaneous

Plum Jam

This is best made with late-ripening plums as these are sweet
and less juicy than the early variety. They can have
small wrinkles at the stalk end.

10 lbs plums
3 lbs sugar
1 cinnamon stick
juice of 1 lemon

Wash and stone the plums and mix them with
the sugar. In a large roasting pan or a large
heatproof dish cook them in the oven set at
350°F until the jam has reached a thick consistency. Stir once in a while. A few minutes before done stir in the lemon juice.Fill
into jars while still hot.

Clarified Butter

In a shallow saucepan, add a large piece of dark bread rind to
3 lbs butter, slowly warm up the butter at low heat, skim off the
foam as it rises and reserve it in a crock. When the butter has
become golden yellow and clear, pour it trough a fine sieve into a clean stoneware jar. ATTENTION: the residue should remain
in the saucepan and be added to the skimmed-off foam; this residue may be used very well in yeast dough recipes. Tightly seal
the jar containing the clarified butter, and store in a cool,
dark place.

"Maibowle"

2 oranges, untreated
1 Tbs sugar
1 small bouquet
woodruff
1 bottle light
white wine
1 small bottle "Sekt"
(sparkling wine)
1/2 bottle club soda

Cut the oranges into 1/5 in. slices. Sprinkle with the sugar and place in a large glass jar. Tie the woodruff with a thread and hang the bouquet from the lip of the jar, leaves downward. Pour 1/2 bottle of the wine over it and put in a cool place to draw for 1-2 hours.
-- Add the other 1/2 bottle of wine, take out the woodruff, and add the "Sekt" and club soda. A light and pleasant drink!

Wild Strawberry "Bowle"

1 lb wild strawberries
(or the small variety
of garden strawberries)
2 oz. sugar
1 bottle red wine,
unchilled
1 bottle white wine,
well chilled
lemon juice
1/2 bottle champagne or
sparkling wine

Use very ripe berries. In a large bowl, sprinkle the strawberries with the sugar, and let them draw for a few hours.
Add 1/2 bottle of the red wine and let the mixture stand, unchilled. Just before serving, add the remaining 1/2 bottle of red wine, and the well-chilled white wine. Sprinkle with a little lemon juice (it brings out the strawberry taste), and lightly mix in the champagne or sparkling wine.

Mulled Wine

Every Christmas market in Bavaria will have a stand selling this drink. Here is a recipe to make it at home:

3 cups red wine
2 Tbs sugar candy
1/2 cinnamon stick
3 cloves
2 orange slices
1 Tbs rum

It is best to prepare this drink in a heatproof glass or china dish. Pour the wine into the dish, add all other ingredients, bring to a boil. Strain, fill in heatproof mugs and serve. A good winter drink!

Mother-In-Law-Tea

3 oranges, untreated
1 lemon, untreated
approx. 3 1/2 oz. sugar
    cubes
juice of 5 oranges
5 Tbs tea leaves
4 cups water
4 Tbs rum

Wash the oranges and the lemon well and rub down the skins with the sugar cubes. Put the orange sugar into a bowl and add the juice of 5 oranges and of the lemon. Stir, cover and let draw for at least 1 hour. Pour the boiling water over the tea leaves, let draw briefly and strain. Mix the tea with the orange juice mixture and the rum and heat it up again. Do not let it boil! Pour into a teapot and serve with Christmas cookies. If there are children in the company, serve the rum separately.

Curdled Milk (Gestöckelte Milch)

In the Alps and in the Bavarian Forest this is a staple item in
every household. It is prepared in small, individual bowls, wider at the rim than at the bottom to
allow the cream to spread nicely.

1 cup fresh, raw milk	Mix the buttermilk or sour milk with the raw milk. Keep in a warm place to set (but not in the sun or on top of the radiator!).
1 Tbs buttermilk or sour milk	

The more rapidly it sets, the better it will taste. Cool briefly
before serving. You may add fruit to taste, e.g., strawberries,
blueberries or raspberries. Some like it sprinkled with sugar
and cinnamon -- others insists on eating it plain, the "natural"
way, with a chunk of dark bread.

Home-made Cottage Cheese

Bavarians distinguish between two types of cottage cheese:
"Topfen" and "Quark". "Topfen", less moist than "Quark", is
more suitable for certain pastries. "Quark", may be
made drier by pressing out the moisture through a clean cloth.
Or you can make your own Topfen, as follows:

4 qts whole milk	In a fireproof dish, mix the milk with the buttermilk or yoghurt. Let stand in a warm place 4-5 hours, to set to a consistency of yoghurt. "Topfen" is best if milk sets fast.
5 Tsp buttermilk or plain yoghurt	

Place dish with set milk into a pan half-filled with water. Heat
to 120°F, until the whey appears. With a knife, cut a diamond into
the substance. Heat again briefly, stirring. Line a sieve with a
linen cloth, pour the hot mixture into it and let drain. Fold the
cloth over the mixture; weight with a plate to press out moisture.
Yields approx. 3/4 lb. Use for all dishes calling for "Topfen".

Andere Bücher aus dem Verlag:

Köstlich frische Salate   von *Olli Leeb*
Das erste Salatbuch, das sich mit allen gewachsenen Salatsorten
befaßt, nach Farben geordnet. Nährwerttabelle, exklusive Farbfotos
von Christian Teubner und viele Zeichnungen, Schutzklappen für die
Seiten.   192 Seiten   ISBN 3-921799-88-0

Schnell was Feines   von *Olli Leeb*
Natürlich frisch, für Dich und mich ... Ein praktisches Rezeptbuch für
Vielbeschäftigte, für den Minihaushalt, für Studenten und Senioren.
Mit vielen Anregungen und Tips. Kalorientabelle. Alphabetische
Anordnung der Rezepte. Schöne Farbfotos von Christian Teubner und
Zeichnungen. Schutzklappen für die Buchseiten.   212 Seiten   ISBN 3-921799-81-3

Ausgewählte Desserts   von *Olli Leeb*
Feine Rezepte für jeden Geschmack und jede Linie. Nach Farben der
verwendeten Früchte geordnet. Farbfotos und reich illustriert. Mit
Nährwerttabelle. Schutzklappen für die Buchseiten.   198 Seiten   ISBN 3-921799-84-8

Bayerische Leibspeisen   zusammengetragen von *Olli Leeb*
300 typische Rezepte aus Altbaiern, Franken und Schwaben, kleine
Bayernkunde und Bayerischer Kalender. Für In- und Ausländer leicht
nachzukochen. Farbfotos und viele Zeichnungen.   172 Seiten   ISBN 3-921799-80-5

Bavarian Cooking   assembled by *Olli Leeb*
Over 300 recipes of old Bavaria, Franconia and Swabia, easy to prepare
at home. Aside from typical Bavarian specialities please note information
about Bavaria, the Bavarians and their customs. Also included you will
find color photos and numerous illustrations.   172 pages   ISBN 3-921799-85-6

Die feinsten Plätzchen-Rezepte   gesammelt von *Olli Leeb*
Das spezielle Backbuch für Plätzchen, Lebkuchen, Guetzli und Konfekt.
Ausgezeichnet mit der Silbermedaille der Gastronomischen Akademie
Deutschlands. Farbfotos, viele Zeichnungen und Schutzklappen für die
Buchseiten.   190 Seiten   ISBN 3-921799-98-8

My favorite Cookies from the Old Country
Loved Recipes assembled by Olli Leeb.
English Edition of "Die feinsten Plätzchen-Rezepte".   190 pages   ISBN 3-921799-97-X

Von früh an fit mit Nico's Kinderküche   von *Olli Leeb*
An Hand dieses Buches können sich Buben und Mädchen ab 10 Jahren
selbständig ein gesundes, schmackhaftes Essen bereiten zur Entlastung
der berufstätigen Mutter. Auch für erwachsene Anfänger geeignet.   80 Seiten   ISBN 3-921799-87-2

Der Fleck muß weg   von *Olli Leeb*
Ein informatives Handbuch zur Pflege, Wäsche und Reinigung edler
Textilien und Lederbekleidung. Ausführliche Materialkunde.   80 Seiten   ISBN 3-921799-86-4

Garment Care   by *Olli Leeb*
Stain Removal easy made.
English Edition of "Der Fleck muß weg".   80 pages   ISBN 3-921799-83-X

Kuchen   von *Olli Leeb*
Jede Menge köstliche Kuchen: Hefeteig-Kuchen, Mürbteig-Kuchen,
Biskuit-Kuchen, Rührteig-Kuchen, Strudelteig und Blätterteig, auch
Kuchen ohne Backen und alternative Kuchen. Schöne Farbbilder und
Zeichnungen. Schutzklappen für die Seiten.   158 Seiten   ISBN 3-921799-70-8

Eva kocht für Adam, Adam kocht für Eva
Gesunde Küche, viele vegetarische Rezepte – ein ideales Buch für die
Zeit nach dem Fasten. Schöne Fotos und viele Zeichnungen.
Mit Schutzklappen für die Seiten.   180 Seiten   ISBN 3-921799-78-3

Rezept-Auslese   aus dem Fundus von *Olli Leeb*
Feine, erprobte Rezepte für Vorspeisen, Salate, Fleisch, Geflügel, Wild,
Fisch und Krustentiere, Beilagen, Gemüse und Desserts. Schutzklappen
für die Buchseiten.   198 Seiten   ISBN 3-921799-68-8